# FIFTY KEY WORDS: THE BIBLE

# 50

# KEY WORDS

## THE BIBLE

by
Julian Charley

LONDON
LUTTERWORTH PRESS

*First published 1971*
LUTTERWORTH PRESS
4 BOUVERIE STREET, LONDON, E.C.4
JOHN KNOX PRESS
RICHMOND, VIRGINIA, U.S.A.

ISBN 0 7188 1769 9

PRINTED IN GREAT BRITAIN BY
RICHARD CLAY (THE CHAUCER PRESS) LTD
BUNGAY, SUFFOLK

# LIST OF WORDS

# INTRODUCTION

When Biblical Word Books abound, some justification for yet another is perhaps warranted. In this case three factors have contributed to its production.

First, there is the sheer fascination of Biblical Word study. I never cease to be amazed at the wealth of material it supplies. Despite variety in Hebrew and Greek usages and the differing emphases of each writer, there is a coherence in these Biblical terms that justifies their being treated as a whole. It is not that the word studied linguistically resolves all further problems, for the meaning must be determined by the context. The *theological* content is the integrating factor.

This leads on, secondly, to the discovery that a selection of Biblical Words produces a compendium of theology, though marked by the limitations of not being systematic and, in this instance, of necessary brevity. The terms constantly interlock. Their mutual dependence is indicated by the use of an asterisk* for reference to another word study. A firm grasp of the main ideas of the major Biblical Words is no mean introduction to theology.

Thirdly, a fresh confidence in the value of expository preaching is an urgent necessity. When so much preaching and teaching have such tenuous links with the Bible or stick persistently to a very limited range of themes, there is a crying need to rediscover the wealth of Biblical ideas. If at least some new lines of thought can be provoked, something will have been accomplished

Julian Charley
St. John's College
Nottingham

1  **ADOPTION** is only occasionally mentioned, but the idea it embodies is basic to much of the teaching of the Bible.

Early practice was coloured by the fact that the Hebrew word for 'father' means 'protector', emphasizing guardianship rather than parenthood. By adopting Eliezer, the childless Abram and Sarai admitted him into the full rights and privileges of the family (Gen. 15: 2–4). In return for the protection offered there were corresponding obligations. When God is described as a father to Israel his son, this is the background (Jer. 3:19): so often the expected response from the son was not forthcoming (Mal. 1:6). It was not a case of fictitious parenthood, but God in his mercy brought Israel under his protection. 'Father of the fatherless and protector of widows' (Ps. 68:5) exactly expresses the idea.

In the Graeco-Roman world adoption frequently was given to a deserving adult. But when God adopts men into his family, they are helpless and undeserving orphans. It is by his gracious choice, not of desert. For all the privilege adoption was for Israel (Rom. 9:4), the people were never allowed to forget their origin (Deut. 26: 5–9). Although occasionally the Bible speaks of God being the father of all men in the sense that he *created* them, it repeatedly teaches that he is father in the fullest sense only to those he has *adopted*. Salvation* begins with justification*, giving men a legal standing before God. It leads on to adoption into the intimate privileges of God's family. Jesus Christ even deigns to call his followers 'brothers' (Heb. 2:11). Such is the goal of God's purpose (Eph. 1:5). We are privileged even to share with Christ the family inheritance (Rom. 8:17). So it is only members of the family that can legitimately pray 'Our Father' (Matt. 6:9). But divine adoption far transcends any human counterpart. Not only are men brought into the family, they are also given 'the Spirit* of adoption' (Rom. 8:15). There is an internal change of heart that radically alters the Christian's attitude. The Spirit prompts him to pray the intimate 'Abba', father. His sonship is no mere alteration of circumstances, but a new life*. 'We *are* sons', says

John: we shall eventually reflect fully the family likeness. In the meantime there is this incentive to live worthily of the family name (1 John 3: 1–3, Matt. 5:48). That sinful men can be called to enjoy by adoption what is Christ's by nature is the marvel of the gospel* – a share in the divine nature (2 Pet. 1:4). That is the measure of the family union envisaged.

2 **BAPTISM** is the outward sign of entry into membership of the church* (1 Cor. 12:13). What circumcision was for the Jew, baptism is for the Christian. It is an unrepeatable initiatory rite. The parallel is drawn in Col. 2:11–12, where Paul shows that in either case it is the spiritual significance that counts. Manifestly no external physical action can of itself bring about an internal spiritual result. God gave these sacramental rites to strengthen faith*, not to replace it. Both were provided as the mark of admission into the covenant*.

When Jesus submitted to the baptism of John, he showed vividly how he would identify himself with men, even to the point of bearing their sin* (Luke 3: 21–2). He spoke of his forthcoming death* on the cross as a baptism (Luke 12:50). What distinguished Christian baptism from that of John was that it was in the name of Jesus Christ and associated with the gift of the Spirit* (Acts 19: 2, 5). It is a sacrament of the gospel* because it portrays the blessings that Christ provides. The first of these is forgiveness* (Acts 2: 38). This is man's* basic need and only God in Christ can bestow it. Past records are wiped clean. But baptism with water also signifies cleansing, for which the Old Testament had good precedent (Ezek. 36:25). Even so, the imagery of the New Testament is more like that of a flood drowning the old life than the washing away of defilement (1 Pet. 3:20–1). In Rom. 6: 3, 4 baptism is described as dying with Christ and rising to a new life, dramatized by entry into the water and emergence from its depths. The putting off of one set of clothing before immersion and the putting on of a new garment afterwards similarly emphasized this radical transformation (Gal. 3:27). The old life was left behind and no longer has any claims upon the baptized. But this change is even more profound than a renunciation of the past. It involves a change of heart within, a washing of regeneration* (Tit. 3:5). For the outward cleansing with water is the counterpart of the inner gift of the Spirit. This is what John the Baptist had promised, just as he had witnessed at the baptism of Jesus (John 1:31–3). To receive the Holy Spirit is the beginning of the Christian life.

However, baptism is no mere option. The risen Christ commanded it (Matt. 28:19). In many lands today baptism still means a decisive step of commitment. John's baptism was a mark of repentance: Christian baptism indicates faith as well (Acts 18:8). Baptism is intended to be a public proclamation of the gospel calling for a public response.

3 **BLOOD:** 'Without the shedding of blood there is no forgiveness of sins' (Heb. 9:22). Why? The answer to this question touches upon the most profound theological themes. It was not because there was any inherent power in the blood itself that God appointed blood sacrifice as the means of atonement for the Israelite. Life* is a creature's most precious possession; therefore the blood may not be eaten, for 'the life of the flesh is in the blood' (Lev. 17:10–11). All life ultimately belongs to God, just as it derives from him. For the Christian, the special importance of the subject stems from the frequent use in the New Testament of 'the blood of Christ' to describe his death.

Two interpretations of this motif have been suggested. First, the emphasis is said to rest not upon the death of the victim but upon the *release* of its life-force resident in the blood. 'The main

3

object is not the slaying of the animal but the release of its life for ceremonial use' (J. A. Wainwright). The death is then regarded as almost incidental. However, this idea of life-release runs counter to basic Hebrew teaching on the nature of man*, besides serious linguistic difficulties.

The second view is that blood emphasizes death* and violent death at that. Man is a combination of flesh and blood (Matt. 16:17). The separation of the two spells death, not the release of an imprisoned life-source, which is a Greek idea. For the Hebrew, life after death was not a spirit-world but an enfeebled kind of bodily existence in Sheol. Similarly the New Testament eagerly anticipates a bodily resurrection* (1 Cor. 15 : 51–2). To be guilty of someone's blood is to be guilty of his death (Matt. 27 : 24–5). This is strongly supported by the special use of the word in Acts 20:26. When Paul says, 'I am innocent of the blood of all of you', he is probably alluding to Ezek. 33, here blood means the judgment of eternal death on the sinner. Atonement is not achieved by the *gift* of a life to God, which would be almost a form of bribery: it is concerned with the exaction of sin's penalty, which God's law requires (Ezek. 18:4). When Christ's blood was shed, his life was not released by his death but by his resurrection (Rom. 5 : 9, 10). The Incarnation was not reversed.

Thus 'the blood of Christ' refers back to the historical events of the Cross. The benefits that stem from Calvary are not only past facts but a vital contemporary experience (e.g. 1 John 1 : 7, and see 'Saint'). When the phrases 'eat my flesh' and 'drink my blood' are combined, they underline the Christian's fellowship with the *whole* Christ, whose death made eternal life possible and whose resurrection guarantees its present reality (John 6 : 52–8). At the Lord's supper this atoning death is commemorated in fellowship with the risen Lord (1 Cor. 10:16). (See also 'Forgiveness', 'Sacrifice'.)

**4 BODY:** The use of terms to describe man's psychological make-up is not entirely uniform, so that each context must be separately assessed. However, there are certain basic principles that form a continuous link. For the Hebrews, body and spirit* are closely integrated. The sharp division between the two ('the body a tomb') is a Greek conception and entirely alien to Biblical thought. The Hebrew attitude, which preferred to speak of 'flesh*' rather than body, is the background to the New Testament. Modern psychosomatic medicine has endorsed the validity of this teaching (see also 'Soul'). A personality needs a body for its full expression: this is the reason for the New Testament emphasis on the resurrection* of the body. Life beyond the grave is not a mere spirit-existence.

Consequently 'body' may often be translated as 'self': 'present your bodies (yourselves) a living sacrifice' (Rom. 12:1). When Jesus spoke of the danger of the 'whole body' being cast into hell, clearly he meant the entire human personality (Matt. 5:30). Paul speaks of the body of sin* and of death* (Rom. 6:6, 7:24), but he does not mean that it is the physical part of man alone that is the seat of evil and mortality. Sin has taken up residence in our earthly frame. Moreover, we are painfully conscious of all the weaknesses and sufferings of body and mind that trouble us on earth. But this 'body of humiliation' is going to be changed (Phil. 3:21). The result will be a permanent transformation that will resemble Christ's glorified state.

Once this significance of the Hebrew idea of the individual's body is grasped, the description of the church* as the body of Christ becomes far more intelligible. Just as a man's body and spirit are not identical, though closely related, neither is the church to be identified with the Spirit of Christ. There is one body and one Spirit (Eph. 4:4). The relationship is very intimate, but the church is not to be understood as *literally* the body of Christ. If it were, then the church would be divine, sinless and able to atone for sins. Nor is the expression a mere pictorial metaphor. It comes somewhere between these two extremes, to

5

describe an organic unity of the profoundest nature without actual identity. Christ fills the body of which he is head with the fulness of God (Eph. 1:22–3).

The unity of the individual personality, despite the diversity of its make-up, is paralleled in the church as the body of Christ. In 1 Cor. 12 Paul emphasizes this diversity in unity. The body has many members, each with a different function but all necessary. Thus there is no place for despising one member and dispensing with it, nor should any feel unwanted or unneeded (vv. 15, 21). Mutual care ought to characterize the members of the body (vv. 24–6).

Contained in this Biblical outlook is a salutary warning against dividing the spiritual and the physical, the sacred and the secular. What God has joined together, let no man put asunder.

5 **CHURCH:** The Greek word *ecclesia*, translated 'church' in the New Testament, is also the word used by the Greek translators of the Old Testament for the 'assembly' of God's people. This link between the two Testaments is important, because it emphasizes the connection between God's people Israel and the Christian church. Also, both the Hebrew and Greek words suggest 'a people summoned together', in this case by God himself. It never means a building, nor must it ever be confused with the ecclesiastical machinery that has overlaid it in subsequent history.

God's people, whether in the Old or New Testaments, have certain distinctive marks. They are *chosen* by him, solely on the grounds of his grace★ (Deut. 7:6–8, 1 Cor. 1:26–9). This removes any cause for boasting. Secondly, they are God's *covenant*★ people, for God enters into a relationship in which he lays down the terms and to which he binds himself (Heb. 8:8–13). Further, they recognize themselves as a *redeemed**★* people (Ex. 6:6, 7). The Israelite was reminded of this at the annual Passover festival; Christians celebrate a still greater Passover deliverance (1 Cor. 5:7). Finally, they are bound together through the covenant into an *united* people (Lev. 19:18). Love★ of his brethren is a hall-mark of the Christian (1 John 3:14).

The history of Israel is a sorry tale of declension, till the prophets have to stress that the true Israel is confined to a godly remnant. It is the spiritual qualities that God requires (Rom. 2:28–9). With the coming of Jesus the Messiah, the watershed is reached. His followers are the true remnant, for now the Christian church takes to itself the very terms used to describe Israel of old (1 Pet. 2:9, 10). When Paul uses the image of the olive tree in Rom. 11:17–20, he shows that the stock remains the same – the fundamentals are spiritual and not organizational or national. The change is in the branches, the individual members.

Repentance★ and faith★ in Jesus Christ are the conditions of membership. Yet it is the Lord himself who adds people to its number (Acts 2:47), for the church is his and he will ensure its triumph (Matt. 16:18). Many metaphors are used to describe the relation of Christ to his disciples in the fellowship★ of the church: the vine and the branches, the shepherd and the flock, the head and the body★, the bridegroom and the bride. They all suggest a deep intimacy and the church's complete dependence upon Christ: some also indicate the inter-dependence of Christians upon one another. To all is committed the dual role of worship and witness. Every Christian exercises the priestly function of offering sacrifices★ and all are Christ's ambassadors (1 Pet. 2:5, 9), though some are given special gifts of leadership in the community (see 'Ministry').

There is only one church, because there is only one body (1 Cor. 12:12, 13). This unity already exists through the Spirit, but it must be maintained in practice (Eph. 4:3–6). All the blemishes that mar the church's life are in process of removal till complete likeness to Christ is finally achieved (Eph. 4:25–7).

**6  COMING:** That God would come and visit his people for the final day of reckoning was the constant expectation of the Old Testament prophets (Is. 2:2-4). Every visitation in history was a further assurance of it. Associated with this 'day of the Lord' was a Messianic figure, a Davidic king or a suffering servant*. Later Jewish speculation found this so baffling that two separate Messiahs were conjectured, the one a king and the other a priest. In fact there was to be one Messiah but two comings, in each of which his primary role would be different. Jesus came first in humility to deal with sin through a priestly sacrifice* of himself. He will come a second time in glory as King, in a manner that will compel all to acknowledge him (Heb. 9:28, Rev. 1:7). The prophetic perspective did not differentiate these comings. Like distant mountain peaks, they look much closer to each other than is really the case. It was a misunderstanding of this that led in part to the people's desire to make Jesus a King (John 6:15).

While it is fundamental that Christ has once come upon earth and that he continues to come to his disciples (John 14:23), the coming of Jesus in the New Testament usually looks ahead to his final return. For the time being Satan still holds sway, even though defeated. The Kingdom* of God slowly spreads, but there will be violent opposition that will culminate in a political figure who will twist religion to his own glorification (2 Thess. 2). These signs before the end will be detected by the disciple*, though the precise hour of the Lord's* return is known only to God (Matt. 24:36). The two main words used to describe this event are significant – *Parousia* was the current term for the arrival in state of a ruler: *Apokalypsis* means 'unveiling', for then there will be a public disclosure of the glory of the exalted Lord (1 Pet. 4:13).

This glorious appearing will be sudden and unexpected, like a thief in the night, and it will be inescapable (1 Thess. 5:1-3). This momentous event will also include the final judgment*. Then will take place the resurrection* of the dead. All will be

8

changed in a moment, both the living and those who have already died (1 Cor. 15:51-4). For the Christian, it means being for ever with the Lord (1 Thess. 4:17). Such an expectation is a constant challenge to abide in Christ that his coming may be a source of joy and not of shame (1 John 2:28).

7 **CONSCIENCE** in the New Testament has a much more precise meaning than its use in everyday speech. It is the internal effect of the revelation of God's wrath★ against sin★ (Rom. 1:18). 'Pangs' of conscience accurately express the idea. This is the pain felt after the commission of a sin; but as in a game where the light flashes on after you have missed the target, so conscience only registers *after* failure. Its role is negative, indicating that some transgression has occurred. Thus a good or clear conscience implies the absence of any consciousness of wrong (Acts 23:1, 24:16). It is a very personal matter, something that literally you 'know with yourself'. This is the reaction of man to the awareness that he has broken a part of the moral law★. Similarly, the Christian is to keep the law of the state so as to avoid both the external punishment of the magistrate and the internal pain of conscience (Rom. 13:5). While conscience is thus negative and retrospective, the mind is able to deliberate on choices beforehand. The two are linked, but distinguished in this way (Rom. 2:14-15). Thoughts may excuse as well as accuse. Of course fallen man may make a wrong choice, since the law★ written on his heart has become blurred. His faculties of discernment need to be trained (Heb. 5:14). 'A good conscience is the absence of this pain from the man who has the capacity to feel it' (C. A. Pierce).

Just as the mind can be darkened, so also the conscience is not an infallible guide. A man's conscience may be 'weak', that is to say 'ill-informed'. This is how Paul described the condition of certain Christians at Corinth concerning meat that had been sacrificed to idols (1 Cor. 8:7). While the mature Christian need not be over-scrupulous on his own account, he must take every precaution that his own knowledgeable action shall in no way mislead the less mature and cause him pangs of conscience (10:25–9). Ignorance or habit produce a 'weak' conscience. It is not to be trampled upon in a superior way, but to be shown considerateness and given instruction.

The tragedy is that the conscience may cease to function properly, if it is constantly stifled. Anyone knows this from experience. It can become defiled (Tit. 1:15) and even cauterized to the extent of complete insensitivity (1 Tim. 4:2). By the mercy of God the pricks of conscience are sometimes sharpened to bring men to faith*. The awareness of past wrong-doings hangs like a mill-stone around the neck, often goading men to frantic good works in order to gain acceptance with God and deliverance. By faith alone is this freedom and cleansing found (Heb. 10:22, 9:14). By faith alone (but an informed faith) can the mind and conscience be restored. But even then, when no pangs are felt, the Christian knows that the final judge of his conduct is not his conscience but God (1 Cor. 4:4).

8 **COVENANT:** Man*, being made in the image of God, has personality. This not only means that he can communicate meaningfully with other men, but supremely that he is capable of a personal relationship with his Maker. The Genesis account clearly shows this (3:8, 9): the tragedy of the Fall was the forfeiting of this potential privilege. With the restoration of this possibility the Bible is primarily concerned. God's method has been to enter into a covenant with man.

Covenants among men were familiar enough. Normally they would involve some mutual contract, with similar or distinct undertakings on either side. Marriage is described in this way

(Mal. 2:14). Yet sometimes a covenant was not on equal terms, but a unilateral declaration. It was for such that the frightened men of Jabesh-Gilead asked: 'Make a treaty with us and we will serve you' (1 Sam. 11:1). When God makes a covenant with man, it is of this nature. He initiates it and he lays down the terms. The Greek translators of the Old Testament recognized this and studiously avoided the obvious Greek word for covenant which implied a mutual agreement.

Thus a covenant originates with God's grace*. It is an undeserved favour bestowed on man. Most of the basic ideas involved are set out in Deut. 7:6–11. The Lord their God loved, chose and redeemed the Israelites. While he is faithful for his part, the people were charged to be careful to observe his commandments. Moreover, the covenant did not attach people individually to their God: the blessings of the covenant were to be enjoyed within the covenant community (v. 6). The same quality of 'covenant-love' that God had demonstrated to them was to characterize their relationships with one another (Mic. 6:8).

In the Old Testament God made covenants with Noah, Abraham, Moses and David. They are in no way opposed to each other or contradictory, for God is not inconsistent. All express God's grace toward man and all are concerned with delivering him from the plight of the Fall. From the promise to all mankind that a flood would not occur again, the divine pledges are narrowed down to a specific people with more precise details, culminating in the promises concerning the line of David which Jesus Christ fulfilled (Luke 1:32–3). Jesus is the originator of the *new* covenant, foretold in Jer. 31:31–4, after which there is a steady expansion as Gentile as well as Jew becomes incorporated in the people of God (1 Pet. 2:10).

This new covenant achieves what the Mosaic covenant was unable to do. The latter had indicated the way of life that was a suitably grateful response for deliverance from Egypt (Ex. 20:2, 3), but the standard of these stone-inscribed laws was a frustratingly impossible target. Now God's laws are written upon the heart and the people of God taught and empowered by the Spirit (Heb. 8:10, 2 Cor. 4:6). All now have access into the very presence of God (Heb. 10:19–22). But a covenant involved a sacrifice\* to seal it and bind both parties together (Ex. 24:6–8): the price was the blood\* of Christ (Mark 14:24). Only in this way could the essence of the covenant be achieved, 'I will be their God and they shall be my people'.

9 **DEATH** is strangely paradoxical. In that we all expect to die, it seems perfectly natural – 'it is appointed for men to die once' (Heb. 9:27). Yet when it occurs, we find it hard to accept simply as a natural event. Our inclination is to resist it as an intruder. This experience is endorsed by what the Bible teaches, for Paul calls it 'the last enemy' (1 Cor. 15:26). He adds that death entered the world\* as the result of sin\* (Rom. 5:12). Whereas we can differentiate between death as a spiritual state and death as a termination of physical existence, the Biblical writers do not draw a hard and fast distinction. The relationship between the two is not explicitly defined. Whether the word refers to a present experience or to a future event must be determined by the context, but frequently both ideas are present.

Consequently death is not to be regarded as merely a natural phenomenon. 'The soul\* that sins shall die' (Ezek. 18:4) is a recurrent theme. When Paul describes it as 'the wages of sin', he means much more than its inevitable consequence (Rom. 6:23). This is God's verdict upon man's sin (Rom. 1:32). It is this causal link between sin and death that makes it so abhorrent. Sin embitters the prospect of death because it emphasizes that death is a punishment that would not exist if man had not rebelled against his Maker. 'The sting of death is sin' (1 Cor. 15:56), for physical death is a judgment\* of God, as well as symbolizing a spiritual experience. Adam died on the day he disobeyed, as God had

12

said (Gen. 2:17); but it was a spiritual death through banishment from his presence: the physical followed later. The speculative question as to what would have occurred if man had not sinned is left unanswered. Since God is the source of spiritual life*, then to be cut off from him is spiritual death – 'dead in trespasses and sins' (Eph. 2:1). Paul can therefore say that death has reigned since Adam's trespass (Rom. 5:17). This is a sphere where the devil* exercises power until all the forces of evil, death included, are finally destroyed at 'the second death' (Rev. 20:10, 14).

Jesus Christ conquered death when he overcame sin and the devil. Spiritually, believers have already passed from death to life (John 5:24). The broken relationship has been restored. In the Old Testament death is regarded as a thick veil; there was little clear revelation of what lay beyond. Now, by the resurrection* of Jesus, death has been abolished (rendered ineffective) and life and immortality brought to light (2 Tim. 1:10). The atonement means that death's sting has been drawn, so that men are delivered from the fear of death (Heb. 2:15). Though believers must still face the weakness and pain that may accompany dying, they need not be afraid of death itself. Just as we still live in an atmosphere of sin, so we continue under the shadow of physical death, though our spirits* are alive (Rom. 8:10). Christ the victor will finally overcome the last enemy also (1 Cor. 15:26, 54–7). Significantly it is Christ and not the devil who at last holds the keys of death and Hades (Rev. 1:18).

10 **DEVIL:** Only too easily we can apply unconsciously to the Devil the attributes which belong to God alone. In the Bible he is always portrayed as an inferior, created being: he is neither omniscient, nor omnipresent, nor omnipotent. In the Greek there is a clear distinction between the Devil, who is one, and the demons, who are many. The origin of this evil company is

13

not explicitly described, but their hierarchy (Eph. 6:12) suggests they are fallen angels, over whom the Devil is the head (Rev. 12:9). Their fall seems to have been caused by pride (1 Tim. 3:6), in forsaking their proper rank and position (Jude 6). Thus the Devil is not a mere influence but a personal being, imbued with an inveterate hostility to God.

Unable to retaliate directly against God, he chose instead to attack his creation, Man*. The Fall displays his set purpose (Gen. 3:1–8); but at that very time God gave a promise of his ultimate defeat by the seed of the woman (Gen. 3:15). Devil means 'slanderer', while Satan means 'adversary' or 'accuser'. His names express his activity, for he has ever accused God before Man (Gen. 3:4, 5) and Man before God (Job 1:9–11, 2:4, 5; Rev. 12:9). Jesus aptly called him 'the father of lies' (John 8:44).

It was to destroy the works of the Devil that the Son of God came into the world (1 John 3:8). In the temptation* in the Wilderness there came a head-on clash (Matt. 4:1–11). His real ambition is revealed in his desire that Jesus Christ should worship him – that same overweening pride that originally caused his downfall. When the Seventy returned, rejoicing that even the demons were subject to them in Christ's name, Jesus said, 'I saw Satan fall like lightning from heaven' (Luke 10:17, 18). Already Satan's usurped kingdom had been invaded and 'the god of this world' defeated (2 Cor. 4:4). At the Cross Jesus Christ publicly triumphed over Satan and all his host (Col. 2:15). By atoning for Man's guilt Christ undid the consequences of Satan's work; by rising again and overcoming 'him who had the power of death', he made freedom from Satan's power a real possibility (Heb. 2:14, 15). It is only the permissive will of God that allows Satan to continue for the present his nefarious work. He knows his days are numbered (Rev. 12:12).

Gehenna, or Hell, is not Satan's chosen abode: it is the place proposed by God into which he has been cast and where, at the last Judgment*, he will be eternally confined (Matt. 25:41). The certainty of this ultimate victory over all the powers of evil is part of the Christian's hope* and a present incentive in the conflict with Satan (a major theme in the Revelation, e.g. 20:10). (See also 'Sin', 'Temptation'.)

11 **DISCIPLE:** To ensure the future diffusion of his message, Isaiah entrusted his teaching to a band of disciples (8:16). The later Rabbinic 'schools' acted similarly, but the function of the teacher was always to expound and apply what God had revealed. Consequently the loyalty of the disciples was primarily to the teaching and not to the teacher. Initially this was how Nicodemus regarded Jesus (John 3:2), but the authority with which he spoke soon showed his uniqueness (3:11; cf. Matt. 7:28-9, John 13:13). Thus to be a disciple of Jesus meant far more than to be a disciple of Gamaliel, because it involved faith* in Jesus Christ as Lord* and submission to his person as well as his teaching (Acts 6:7). It is significant that the disciples are often called 'his' in the Gospels, which emphasizes this relationship.

The beginning of discipleship is not simply a human choice. It is a response to the summons, 'Follow me' (Mark 1:17). The very idea of discipleship might convey an impression of the priority of academic knowledge*, but nothing could be further from the truth. The first disciples were not notable for their intellectual gifts. They were mainly simple folk who had often to be upbraided for their slowness to learn. Dedication to Jesus and his mission was the prime requirement. It has ever been the mistaken desire of men to separate the teaching of Jesus from this personal loyalty, but the former is unattainable without the latter. Here lies the uniqueness of Christianity, for which a right understanding of discipleship is an invaluable safeguard. Even the apostles never ceased to be disciples, since none can ever get beyond this position of dependence.

Nevertheless, the disciple is always a learner too – learning ho to live. This is practical and not theoretical. The more he learns, the more like Christ he should become (Luke 6:40). But this training is not for self-gratification. The disciple is both to spend time at the feet of the Teacher and to go out on whatever mission he is sent (Mark 3:14). Evangelism involves sharing with others the teaching received and leading them in their turn to become disciples (Matt. 28:19, 20). He has the assurance of his Master's spiritual presence and the incentive of his future return (Luke 12:35-8). In the meantime he must sort out his loyalties and prepare for suffering (Luke 14:26-7). In aligning himself with Jesus, he cannot avoid a share in the treatment meted out to his Master (Matt. 10:24-5).

12 **ELECT:** The Old Testament writers were convinced that God had chosen Israel rather than that Israel had chosen God.

Behind this doctrine of election lie several vital theological truths. First, it underlines the fact that God is omnipotent (Ps. 29:10). Everything is ultimately under his control and he is free to act as he pleases. Secondly, it is a reminder that God has a purpose for everything (Prov. 16:4). History has a goal towards which he leads it unerringly. Thirdly, election is an act of God's grace*. When Israel tried to explain the reason for their being chosen, they could only say that it was totally undeserved. Neither their righteousness nor their numerical strength were the cause, but only the love* of God (Deut. 9:4, 5; 7:7, 8). Election brought them into the privileges of being the covenant* people of God, with all the corresponding obligations. Thus election always has a corporate aspect, but even in the Old Testament there are the beginnings of an individual emphasis. The 'godly remnant' suggests the distinction between being chosen for the privileges of membership of the people of God and election to the enjoyment of the personal relationship with God himself which is real life* (Ps. 65:4, Is. 10:20, 21).

Election does not mean that man ceases to be a responsible

16

moral agent. He must make his own choice also (Deut. 30:15–20). Man's freedom is never absolute but always relative. Christian experience endorses these two seemingly opposed choices, God's and man's. In retrospect the Christian sees that his decision to follow Christ was preceded by God's election (John 15:16, Eph. 1:4). God 'draws', man 'comes' (John 12:32, 5:40). The invitation is extended more widely than the election, which will reveal itself in holiness of life (Matt. 22:14, 2 Pet. 1:10).

The sovereignty of God is borne out by the associated ideas of foreknowledge and predestination*, each a reminder that God knows the end from the beginning. Election exalts God's grace in such a way as magnifies human helplessness and sin*. For the Christian this brings a deep sense of assurance, because God's choice is 'in Christ' and therefore eternal (Eph. 1:4). There is a progression to a share in God's glory that is guaranteed (Rom. 8:28–30). Far from encouraging pride or laziness, this acts as a spur to holiness and service. The danger of presumption was recognized by Paul (Rom. 11:19–22), but once the implications of election are really grasped there can be no place for anything but humble gratitude.

13 **FAITH** or 'believing' recurs frequently throughout the Bible because it expresses the only acceptable attitude of man towards God, of which Abraham is the outstanding example (Gen. 15:6). The root of the Hebrew word means 'stability'. From this it follows that a confidence in the everlasting and unchanging God imparts something of that steadfastness to the believer (Is. 26:3, 4). It involves a self-abandoning, total commitment.

Greek usage suggests three stages in faith. First, there is belief in a *fact* (1 John 5:1). It is important to emphasize this because Christian faith is not an irrational leap in the dark. No one is expected to have faith without prior evidence, which concerns the person and work of Christ. Commitment necessitates an acceptance of these basic facts: it does not require an elaborate creed initially (Rom. 10:9), though personal faith in Christ will lead on to full acceptance of his trustworthiness in every sphere. Secondly, there is belief in someone's *word* (John 4:21). God has not only recorded for us certain facts but also their interpretation, so faith must proceed to accept the significance of those facts. Similarly, the listener may acknowledge the truth of the preacher (Acts 8:12). But neither of these stages so far is adequate to constitute a 'saving' faith, whereby a man is transferred from Satan's control to God's (Acts 26:18). This final stage is trust in a *person*, in Christ himself (John 3:16). When facts and interpretation are accepted, there should follow this complete commitment. It results in an intimate union with Christ; He becomes the firm foundation of the believer's life. Moreover, everlasting life* is the Christian's immediate, present possession (John 5:24). This step of faith is no mere fatalism, because it involves a real personal relationship. Nor does it imply a sort of passive resignation, since it issues in an active struggle against all evil (1 Tim. 6:12). This is why faith and obedience are closely associated (Rom. 10:16). What must begin with a definite act must also continue in an unchanging attitude. The Christian never grows out of the need for faith.

Confidence in God grows with awareness of his faithfulness (Rom. 3:3). Nothing can possibly alter that. Through the work of the Spirit* a Christian is to become dependable like his Lord, but never independent (Gal. 5:22). To some is given a special gift, which probably implies a particular vocation to 'live by faith' (1 Cor. 12:9). The Christian message is called 'the faith' because it is taken on trust from God himself (James 2:1).

So fundamental is all this that 'believers' becomes a regular term for Christians. They have learned to walk by faith and not by sight until they see their Master face to face (Heb. 11:1). Faith receives what grace* bestows. There is no merit in faith, only in its object. 'There cannot be a more humble soul than a believer.

It is no pride in a drowning man to catch hold of a rock' (Samuel Rutherford).


14 **FELLOWSHIP** is a welcome word to the lonely and isolated. It is fundamental to an understanding of the church★.

While in New Testament times the word as often as not referred to a business partnership, the apostles imported into it a new wealth of meaning. Fellowship binds together. Its primary emphasis is on sharing in something, often together with other people. The result is to want to give to others a share in what we enjoy.

Now Christian fellowship has no parallel because it is a sharing in God. We have fellowship with the Father, the Son and the Spirit★ (1 John 1:3, 1 Cor. 1:9, 2 Cor. 13:14). This is not only a knowledge★ of God, nor even a personal relationship with him: we become partakers of the divine nature (2 Pet. 1:4). Something of the significance of this can be deduced from Jesus' parable of the vine and the branches. 'Abide in me and I in you'. This is not a kind of pantheism whereby men are swallowed up in the Divine Being. On the contrary, it is a mutual relationship in which human identity is retained, but where life★ is transformed by a spiritual union. This is the Christian's legal standing 'in Christ'. It is his present experience because God has given his Spirit to dwell in him (Rom. 8:1, 9). It will reach its culmination when he sees his Lord★ face to face (1 Cor. 13:12).

Such fellowship with God necessarily involves not only a share in the blessings of the gospel★, but also a joint participation in its spread (Phil. 1:5). This testimony to the truth inevitably incurs a share in Christ's sufferings as a witness, in which Christians participate together (2 Cor. 1:5–7). For we are not simply bound to the Lord in fellowship by individual threads, but in the process closely knit together with one another. The New Testament first coined many 'together' words to express this –

fellow-soldier, fellow-citizen, fellow-servant. The fellowship is God's family. Consequently the welcoming right hand of fellowship is the natural attitude towards Christian brothers (Gal. 2:9). It was this refusal to welcome the brethren, even fellow-workers, that made the conduct of Diotrephes so odious (3 John 5–10). 'If God so loved us, we also ought to love one another' (1 John 4:11). This expression of love will not be mere emotion but must issue in concrete action. Financial relief for the poor Christians was undertaken by Paul and warmly shared by those able to help (2 Cor. 8:4, 9:13). Here the actual word is almost synonymous with generosity.

It is at the Lord's table that fellowship with Christ and with one another are especially brought into focus (1 Cor. 10:16–7). That is why a man should examine himself before taking part. This privileged fellowship must not be presumed upon but jealously guarded. Christian unity already exists but it must be kept intact (Eph. 4:3). Its blessings do not just happen: we must 'devote ourselves' to it (Acts 2:42). To walk in the light is God's appointed way (1 John 1:6, 7). (See also 'Body'.)

15 **FLESH:** Besides its obvious meaning, flesh can denote the entire human being. Thus it is often a synonym for 'people' (Is. 40:5). The intimacy of marriage constitutes two people one flesh (Gen. 2:24). In the Old Testament, flesh particularly contrasts man's weakness with the strength of the Spirit* of God (Is. 31:3). This is the spring-board for the New Testament's fully developed doctrine.

Again, flesh means people (1 Cor. 1:29 RSV). Jesus stressed its characteristic weakness to the disciples* in Gethsemane (Mark 14:38). But the New Testament explains this weakness at much greater depth. This is where sin* and death* have gained a foothold. The whole of human nature has become contaminated,

20

so that Paul can say, 'Nothing good dwells within me, that is, in my flesh' (Rom. 7:18). Not that it is sinful to be *in* the flesh, since God himself was manifested in that way (1 Tim. 3:16). God sent his Son 'in the likeness of sinful flesh', genuinely man but without the taint of sin (Rom. 8:3). What is condemned is to live *according* to the flesh, fulfilling its promptings (Rom. 8:5, 6). This is neither a condemnation of sex nor an advocacy of asceticism. (See also 'Body'.)

When a man becomes a Christian, he receives the Spirit into his inner being: without the Spirit, he does not belong to Christ at all (Rom. 8:9). Christ is formed in him, lives in him (Gal. 4:19, 2:20). But he is still 'in the flesh' and in danger of succumbing to its suggestions, unless he takes special care (Rom. 13:14). Paul's list of the outworkings of the flesh in Gal. 5:19-21 proves that flesh means much more than what we normally imply by carnality. It is precisely because the flesh continues so long as we live on earth that we will never attain sinless perfection here and now. That is why the Christian longs for the redemption* of his body*, for at the resurrection* it will *not* be one of flesh (Rom. 8:23, 1 Cor. 15:49-50). This is the fulfilment still awaited.

But this does not mean that the Christian must adopt an attitude of resignation and expect constant defeat. On the contrary, he need not give in to the flesh's desires. He has become a battle-ground between the Spirit of Christ and the flesh, and they are diametrically opposed (Gal. 5:17). Since Christ condemned sin in the flesh, it no longer has any rightful claim upon the believer (Rom. 8:3, 6:12). When the Christian exhibits the works of the flesh, such as jealousy and strife, he is acting like other men, as if the flesh were still master; but Christians are not 'ordinary men' (1 Cor. 3:1-3). Christ by his Spirit can enable them to overcome the downward pull of the flesh (Rom. 8:2, Gal. 5:16). Instead of the old selfcentredness there will appear a character resembling that of their Master (Gal. 5:22-3).

**16 FORGIVENESS** lies at the heart of Christianity. In that a right relationship with God is the fundamental human need, forgiveness is the blessing that brings in all others. Since sin★ is primarily an offence against God, it is he who must forgive. If he does not, man's lot is hopeless; but there *is* forgiveness with God (Ps. 130: 3, 4). Somewhat surprisingly, the Psalmist adds that this will lead to fear of the Lord★. This is no slavish terror, but the awe and wonder of the pardoned sinner. Whereas the guilt of sin has a profoundly depressing effect psychologically, forgiveness produces relief and freedom. Such an act of God's grace★ evokes a response of grateful love★. 'God does not treat the man as he deserves. But does love anywhere do that?' (H. R. Mackintosh). Far from prompting moral laxity, the ethical influence of forgiveness is all the greater for its not being primarily concerned with the moulding of character. 'We love, because he first loved us' (1 John 4: 19).

A holy God cannot lightly pardon sin. Forgiveness is a costly thing, for an offence cannot be simply overlooked: the penalty must be paid. Even if God had 'passed over' former sins in his mercy, ultimately Christ was to expiate them (Rom. 3:24, 25). The divine love is a holy love, necessitating on God's side the act of atonement and on man's an attitude of penitence and faith★, though even these are God's gift (Ex. 34:6, 7). There is a finality about the forgiveness of God. It is not given by degrees; such a process would only lead to a fresh type of legalism, a mode of earning God's favour. When sin is pardoned, it is permanently removed (Ps. 103:12). It is unthinkable that we should request God's forgiveness while refusing to forgive those who have offended us (Matt. 6:15). Our own experience of God's mercy must colour our attitude towards others (Eph. 4:32).

Forgiveness is far more than the cancellation of a penalty. It draws the sinner into an intimate relationship with God. The sense of assurance that we are pardoned stems from the enjoyment of his presence. Disobedience in the Christian does not terminate his being a child of God, but it does damage the relationship.

22

Any disruption of that fellowship★ will be immediately corrected on confession of the sin that caused it (1 John 1:9).

**17  GOSPEL:** The Roman world hankered after 'good news'. To meet this demand, the imperial cult evolved. Because the emperor was accorded divine honours, his accession to the throne would produce such a proclamation. So would news of a victory, for which 'gospel' was the usual word in secular Greek. In such a context the Christians proclaimed the unique gospel of the Kingdom★ of God. It was a message about Jesus Christ, the real divine Saviour that men awaited. Therefore there could be no other gospel: to tamper with it would destroy it (Gal. 1:6, 7). The coming of Jesus meant 'good news of a great joy', as the shepherds were told (Luke 2:10). It was for this that the Old Testament saints★ had been eagerly waiting.

From the start of his preaching ministry, Jesus showed an awareness of the significance of his coming, and his preaching rang with a note of good news (Mark 1:14-15). Those three years were largely confined to ministry among the Jewish people, but after the resurrection and ascension to his heavenly throne, the gospel would be proclaimed to all the Gentile nations also (Mark 13:10). Yet this very message will be an offence to those who want dramatic signs or clever arguments (1 Cor. 1:21-3). Not that either are lacking; but men do not find God on their own terms, for salvation★ involves far more than superstitious awe or academic exercises. Since the Gospel is God's word to man (1 Cor. 2:9, 2 Cor. 5:20), it must be obeyed (Rom. 10:16). Good news it is, but it makes demands also. Christian conduct must be worthy of such a message (Phil. 1:27). This is no cleverly devised fable of man's imagining. It is a revelation from God himself (Gal. 1:11-12). Even its faithful proclamation will not automatically take effect, unless God

23

personally reveals it to the individual and he responds in faith* (2 Cor. 4:3, Heb. 4:2).

From the Acts of the Apostles we can deduce what this message contained. 'The Old Testament prophecy is fulfilled and the new age has dawned with the coming of Christ. As foretold, he died to deliver us and was raised on the third day, exalted to God's right hand as Lord*. He will come again as Judge and Saviour'. This gospel is emphatically 'according to the scriptures', not a contradiction of God's earlier dealings with men. The cardinal facts are the death and resurrection* of Jesus (1 Cor. 15:3, 4). So the good news is firmly rooted in history, but the proclamation also explains the significance of the events. The death was sacrificial, 'for our sins'*: the resurrection indicated the authority he now wields (Rom. 1:3, 4). Resurrection, exaltation as Lord and Judgment* are closely associated. The Saviour who died is the living Lord who reigns. The whole message is good news for man that God is in control and has come to the rescue. Because the gospel expresses God's purpose, it *is* the very power of God to save men (Rom. 1:16). Because of the finality of Christ, the message is eternally valid and eternally the same (Rev. 14:6). Such a sacred trust may not be treated lightly (1 Tim. 1:11).

**18  GRACE** is supremely the key word of the Bible. It is the quality repeatedly ascribed to God in his dealings with men* (Ex. 34:6, Acts 20:24). Grace implies the action of a superior to an inferior. More than this, every gracious expression of kindness and mercy is totally undeserved (Lam. 1:18, 3:22). Because of human sin*, if there were no grace, there would be no hope*. Grace is God in action for the salvation* of sinful men. Since God's way of rescuing sinners involves making a covenant* with them, grace may be defined as 'covenant-love'. Such a love* chooses the undeserving, saves them and keeps them. All is of

24

grace from beginning to end. Grace and mercy are frequently linked: whereas mercy represents God's pity for the weak and helpless, grace speaks of his pardoning love for the sinful and erring. In a derivative sense, man's response to God and attitude to his fellows should reflect the same quality (Hos. 6:6, Mic. 6:8).

Nowhere is the grace of God more manifest than in Jesus Christ (Acts 15:11). Even so, in the New Testament it is the grace of God the Father that is most often mentioned. The reason for this is plain. Salvation begins with divine election* (Gal. 1:15), the Father's sovereign choice and initiative. Even conversion itself is wholly attributable to God's grace, without detracting in any way from human responsibility (John 6:44). The whole process is God's free gift to which our good deeds contribute nothing (Eph. 2:8, 9). Even faith* (Phil. 1:29) and repentance* (Acts 11:18) are given us by God. The conclusion of all this is the total exclusion of boasting: we owe everything to Jesus Christ (1 Cor. 1:30-1). What appears paradoxical is nevertheless endorsed by Christian experience, as D. M. Baillie vividly described it: 'When I make the wrong choice, I am entirely responsible, and my conscience condemns me. And yet (here is the paradox) when I make the right choice, my conscience does not applaud and congratulate me'. This is what Paul affirms in 1 Cor. 15:10. Our responsibility lies in co-operation with God's grace that it may not be in vain (2 Cor. 6:1). Grace glorifies God and not man.

Two misconceptions need to be removed. First, it is possible to set up a false antithesis between law* and grace. Both have their place under the old and the new covenants. The Prologue to the Fourth Gospel does not place them in opposition but in contrast (John 1:17). The law was *given*, an impersonal thing unable to empower its recipients: grace *came* in the person of Jesus Christ, able to save to the uttermost (Heb. 7:25). Bondage through inability is replaced by freedom through power, but the Christian is still under law to Christ (1 Cor. 9:21). The second misconception, often associated with the sacraments, is that grace is a supernatural gift or endowment: it becomes depersonalized. When grace suggests power, as in 2 Cor. 12:9, it is not to be thought of as something distinct from Christ himself. A growing knowledge of him will involve a deeper experience of his grace (2 Pet. 3:18). (See also 'Justification'.)

**19 HOPE** in everyday use expresses an optimistic view of the future, even when its fulfilment is very uncertain. Such an illusion must be created to make life tolerable. How striking a contrast to this is found in the Biblical outlook, for here hope and faith* are intimately related and they are both focused upon God. If he is utterly reliable now, such will he continue into the future. For the servant of the Lord there *is* a definite future (Jer. 29:11, Prov. 23:18). Therefore, although hope involves an element of expectation and waiting, it is grounded upon complete confidence in the Lord of history. The believer's hope is no blind optimism but an assured certainty.

That is why it can be said that the heathen have no hope (Eph. 2:12), because they live without the God who can alone ensure it. That is why a religion that depends on the achievements of man rather than upon the grace of God never produces hope. An eminent Rabbi, Johanan ben Zakkai, a contemporary of the Apostles, said on his death-bed, 'Two paths are before me, the one leading to the Garden of Eden, the other to Gehenna, and I do not know along which path they are taking me – why then should I not weep?' Such was the tragic result of legalistic Judaism.

The *source* of the Christian's hope is the living God (1 Tim. 4:10). His past activities are recorded in the Old Testament scriptures for our encouragement that God is working his purpose out, despite all signs to the contrary (Rom. 15:4). But what the Jew of those days did not know has now been disclosed in the

Gospel★ of Jesus Christ. The New Testament emphasizes the Resurrection★ as the ground of the Christian's hope – the culmination of Christ's saving work on earth – because by this has been dispelled the cloud that obscured a clear vision of the next life during Old Testament times (1 Pet. 1:3, 2 Tim. 1:10).

The *content* of the Christian's hope is manifold. Its fulfilment will be inaugurated by Christ's return (Tit. 2:13). The Christian eagerly anticipates the privilege of being ushered into the very presence of God to share in the glory★ that was forfeited by the Fall (Rom. 5:2). Then, too, he will receive a resurrection body that will be a perfect vehicle for the service of God (2 Cor. 5:1-5, 1 Thess. 4:13). This will be the consummation of man's salvation,★ the transforming vision of God face to face (1 John 3:2).

The *fruit* of the Christian's hope is an unshakeable confidence in the face of all adversity. With the Spirit★ as the guarantee of what lies in store, he knows that he will not be disappointed (Rom. 5:5). He can afford to be patient (Rom. 8:25). Moreover, such a prospect acts as a spur to holiness, to be ready for that day (1 John 3:3). Far from being escapism, hope produces a clearer perspective and so nerves a man to face life's challenge without flinching.

20 **JUDGMENT:** A sense of 'fair play' is a deeply entrenched human instinct: it accounts for the whole system of Law★.

But whereas man's attitude to justice is frequently selfish, the Biblical view is entirely God-centred. God is Judge (Gen. 18:25).

No other group of words is more often used in the Old Testament to describe the nature of God than that which expresses the ideas of justice. He is both King and Judge (Ps. 99:1-4), for it is not enough merely to give a decision. There must be the power to see that it is enforced. This is borne out by the constant refrain in the Book of Judges: 'In those days there was no King in Israel; every man did what was right in his own eyes'.

Now the task of the Judge was to sift evidence. The sifting of evidence must precede the sifting of men. It is compared to the process of winnowing (Prov. 20:8). This idea of separating good from bad is fundamental to the Biblical usage. It would be quite wrong to stress only the negative side of punishment for the evil-doer. The defence and deliverance of the oppressed is equally important (Ps. 72:1-4). So it is with God. His judgment is a continuing, constructive process of sifting men, that will reach its culmination in the 'Day of the Lord'. Not only does he give a wholly just verdict; he alone can ensure that it is duly carried out.

Many of the parables of Jesus carry this same thought – the sheep and the goats, the wheat and the tares. But the New Testament clarifies the picture further. It speaks of both a present and a future judgment. The *present* judgment turns upon men's reaction to the coming of Jesus Christ into the world. For most, darkness was preferable to light (John 3:19). The nature of men's response to Christ divides them one from another; the only true response is one of faith\*. Thus *faith* is the crucial issue in the present judgment.

But there is to be a *future* judgment as well, corresponding to the Old Testament expectation of the 'Day of the Lord'. Christ will be the Judge, all will be involved, reward and punishment will be administered (2 Cor. 5:10). This will be the day of public vindication of God's justice in separating sheep from goats, believer from unbeliever. It will not be to decide who are the true believers; that will have been settled already in this life (John 5:24). This is why the future judgment is always concerned with men's *works* rather than with their faith, as for instance in Matt. 25:31-46. As James repeatedly says, a faith that does not show itself in good works is not genuine. In that day all will have to acknowledge the inescapable, proven fact that 'God's judgments are true and just'.

**21  JUSTIFICATION:** The justice of God is a dominant theme in the Bible, without which both Old and New Testaments lack any real coherence. The Reformers rediscovered this significance, still so often obscured. Not so long ago William Temple wrote of the danger of 'a conception of God so genially tolerant as to be morally indifferent'. Now justification is a metaphor drawn from the law-court: God is judge. Instead of a picture of harshness, it portrays a God of infinite compassion, though one who will never compromise his holiness. Once it is seen that all men stand guilty before God without any excuse to offer, the hopelessness of the situation becomes clear. From one angle there is the anguished cry of Job, 'How can a man be just before God?' (9:2). Or again, there is the theological problem of how God can both remain just and yet justify sinful men (Rom. 3:26). The astonishing message of the gospel★ is that God has done the very thing which the Old Testament said was an abomination to him: he has justified the ungodly (Prov. 17:15, Rom. 4:5). Through the coming of Christ it is now possible for God to pass a verdict of acquittal upon sinners without any breach of justice. (See 'Judgment'.)

To justify means to declare innocent or righteous. It does not mean to *make* righteous. Yet this is no legal fiction, for the Christian has become united with Christ. He is now accepted 'in Christ', where he enjoys both a new status and a new life★. In one of the most profound verses in the New Testament Paul explains that there has taken place a mutual exchange: the sinless Christ took our sin★ that we sinful men might receive God's righteousness★ (2 Cor. 5:21). The Christian is acquitted because he is now looked upon as in Christ, who has atoned for his sins and made possible that ultimate perfection of righteousness.

The Christian is said to be justified in four ways. First and foremost, he is justified by God's grace★ (Rom. 3:24). It is a free gift and totally undeserved, to which he can make no contribution whatever. Secondly, this justification was achieved through Christ's blood★, the atoning death upon the cross (Rom. 5:9).

It was no mere martyr's fate that Jesus sought by refusing to escape the road to Calvary. But this gift, so dearly won, must be appropriated; justification is also through faith* (Rom. 5:1). Faith is not the ground of justification but the means of securing it. Lastly, James stresses the need for good works as evidence that a man is justified (James 2:24). The fact that Paul and James both take Abraham as an illustration of faith and works respectively suggests they are not contradictory. What James warns against is a barren orthodoxy. Acceptance with God must issue in a transformed life, but without faith it will not follow.

22 **KINGDOM** suggests to us a territorial area, but the Biblical words almost invariably stress the sovereignty of the ruler rather than the place over which he rules. To speak of the Kingdom of God is equivalent to saying, 'God is King' (Ps. 103:19). The theme re-echoes throughout the whole of the Bible. It was central to the message of Jesus himself (Mark 1:15). In Judaism the fear of using God's name lightly had resulted in the substitution of alternative words; thus 'kingdom of heaven', as in Matthew's gospel, means the same as 'kingdom of God'.

For the rabbis, God's kingly rule was only extended in the present when men submitted to 'the yoke of the law*'. Only in the final Day of the Lord would God intervene to establish his authority conclusively. But Jesus proclaimed that with his coming the kingdom of God had invaded the present in an unique way, without eliminating the need to pray for its future completion (Matt. 4:17, 6:10). Men were called to submit to *his* yoke instead (Matt. 11:29). Of course God had been upon the throne all along, as the Psalms frequently assert. The patriarchs had been able to enter the kingdom (Luke 13:28), so that this was nothing new. What *was* significant and unexpected was this divine intervention before the final consummation of all things. By his complete subservience to the Father's will, Jesus was the embodiment of the kingdom. It was only to be expected therefore that

30

his ministry would demonstrate unique power, as his miracles* disclosed – the implication should have been obvious (Luke 11:20). But the kingship of Jesus was opposed by a rival sovereignty. Satan also exercised a dominion among men (Matt. 12:26). It was to deliver men from this bondage that Jesus came. Although it can be seen from this that the kingdom of God comes to us, that the initiative is on God's side, nevertheless a response is called for. To enter the kingdom is to experience eternal life*, and both are the result of submitting to the kingship of Jesus Christ (Mark 9:45-7). This is God's gift, bestowed on those who acknowledge their spiritual poverty and respond with child-like faith* (Luke 12:32, Matt. 5:3, 19:14). That Jesus has made this available is surely 'good news'.

The response that men are told to make to this gospel* is to seek the kingdom (Luke 12:31). It is not an offer to the casual, but to those who are in earnest. Repentance* is essential, for the quality of life required within the kingdom demands the highest standards (e.g. Matt. 18:23-35). Many obstacles impede entry, such as a wealth that breeds self-confidence (Luke 18:24-5). This explains the fact that the coming of the kingdom brings judgment*, since God's offer may be accepted or refused. Only in the last day will this division be finalized. Then every rival claimant to God's throne will have to acknowledge Jesus Christ as 'King of Kings' (Rev. 19:16), before he ultimately delivers up the kingdom to the Father.

23 **KNOWLEDGE** to the Greek was essentially intellectual, a detached, impersonal learning, whose opposite was ignorance. For the Hebrew, while he would not deny this intellectual aspect, it meant far more. Knowledge involved experience and a share in the object of interest. Thus a man* may 'know' the loss of children or 'know' a woman (Is. 47:8, Gen. 4:1). When the object of knowledge is God, its opposite is independence and disobedience. Knowledge spells involvement, whether it be

God's concern with his people or the Israelites' relationship with God (Hos. 13:5, 2:20). Man has a basic duty to know God, which implies both an understanding of who he is and what he requires as well as a commitment to serve him accordingly (Jer. 9:24). It is this much wider use of the word that is taken over into the New Testament. That is why John can speak of both knowing and doing the truth (1 John 2:21, 1:6).

Supremely in the New Testament knowledge is focused upon Jesus Christ. Eternal life* is this experiential knowledge of him, which is to progress and deepen (John 17:3, 2 Pet. 3:18). Inevitably it involves a mental grasp of the facts about his nature and his work, together with a complete submission to him in faith*. No one can attain this through his own efforts. The first move must be God's gracious act of revelation (Matt. 11:27).

The early Christians had to combat two false ideas of knowledge and the conflict can be read between the lines of the New Testament. One regarded this knowledge of God as an intellectual, philosophical attainment. The other treated it as an esoteric revelation given to the few and bearing little relation to moral conduct. In either case the door of knowledge was closed to the majority of mankind, whereas the gospel* was open to all, including the simplest (1 Cor. 1:26, 27). There is a wisdom and knowledge that is pure and peaceable, but the dangers of intellectual arrogance always threaten (James 3:13–17, 1 Cor. 8:1). So long as there is kept in view the fact that all the treasures of wisdom and knowledge are hidden in Christ, a safeguard against pride and error is maintained (Col. 2:3).

24 **LAW** is expressed in many different words in Hebrew, but the key term is 'Torah', which means 'instruction'. This is used technically for God's instruction, thus underlining its divine authority. Consequently the teacher of the law had a solemn obligation (Mal. 2:7). The separate instructions are compre-

hended in the single Torah of the Pentateuch. This was given to the Israelites *after* God had entered into a covenant* with them and redeemed* them. It was to be the response of a grateful people for God's gracious dealings (Ex. 20:2, 3); it was emphatically *not* the means of becoming God's people. To observe the law was the appointed way to enjoy the blessings of the covenant and not to forfeit the privileges of that relationship: that is why so many of the laws are prohibitions. After the Babylonian exile the Jews tended to regard the mere possession of the law as constituting them God's people. Instead of being the pattern for showing their indebtedness, it came to be regarded as a means of gaining acceptance with the Lord. This abuse of the law accounts for the apparent contradiction in the New Testament, when the law appears to be both accepted and rejected.

If Moses was the agent for providing the original Torah, Jesus is the new law-giver. In Matt. 5 his repeated 'But *I* say to you' applies the meaning of the law to the innermost motives of the heart. He did not come to destroy the law: not even its smallest letter would be discarded till all was fulfilled (vv. 17 and 18). By submitting himself to it, he was acknowledging that it was good in itself, while he obeyed it at every point. Its weakness lay outside of itself in the powerlessness of human nature to observe it (Rom. 7:22–3). The two things that the law could not do, God made possible by the gift of his Son and of his Spirit (Rom. 8:1–4). By his death, once for all, Christ has *justified*\* us, so that the sacrificial system has been fulfilled and superseded. By the Spirit God is *sanctifying* us so that the law may be fulfilled in our daily lives (see 'Saint'). Consequently its moral requirements still stand for the Christian, but they are now written on the heart to enable us both to know and to practise them (Heb. 8:10).

The Israelites under the law had been like an immature child under the tutelage of a specially appointed household slave (Gal. 3:24). When Christ came, they were to enter the full privileges of the adult son by putting their faith* in him. The law exposed sin* and sought to prepare men to welcome the Saviour

33

(Rom. 7:7, 11). Previously there had always been a sense of incompleteness and bondage: now the Christian is under grace* (Rom. 6:14). The Spirit has 'interiorized' the law, making its observance a possibility on a deeper level, with none of the dread that prevailed before Christ's coming*. Love* is the fulfilment of the law (Rom. 13:10) and this is what God has shed abroad in our hearts.

25 **LIFE:** That God is the living God is frequently attested (e.g. Jos. 3:10), in stark contrast to the idols of the heathen (Is. 44:9-20). 'As the Lord lives' was a common form of oath. All life stems from God and remains dependent upon him (Ps. 104:27-30). But though man* shares physical life with the rest of the animal creation, it is very plain that for him it has a much deeper significance. Made in the image of God, he is described in such a way that differentiates him from all other creatures (Gen. 2:7). This means much more than an advanced stage on the evolutionary scale, as it might be expressed today. It concerns primarily the potentiality for a relationship with God of a personal nature. Man does not live by bread alone; he needs God's self-communicating Word for the real fulfilment of his life (Deut. 8:3). This higher level involves obedience* to the revelation God gives and love* for the giver (Deut. 30:20).

The possibility of life at two levels comes out explicitly in the teaching of Jesus (Matt. 16:25-6). It is possible for a man to live as if he were no more than an animal, but this bare existence falls far short of the life God intends him to enjoy. No doubt the rich young ruler sensed this when he asked, 'What must I do to inherit eternal life?' (Mark 10:17-22). Jesus' answer elaborated the second part of the Ten Commandments, applying it where it hurt, and he concluded, 'Follow me'. Life on the highest level necessitates a right relationship with both God and man. The

34

young ruler may have envisaged something in the future in the Messianic age, but eternal life begins now.

As a result of the Fall, man was barred from the tree of life (Gen. 3:22). Adam could only transmit physical life to posterity: the last Adam, Jesus Christ, became a life-giving spirit* on an entirely different level (1 Cor. 15:45). The Jews mistakenly thought that the mere possession of the scriptures guaranteed them eternal life, when all the time those very writings pointed to Jesus as its source, to whom they were unwilling to turn (John 5:39, 40). This life is his gift and, once given, will not be taken away (John 10:28). It is an abundant, overflowing experience of the living God (John 10:10). In this very context Jesus at once speaks of the Good Shepherd laying down his life for the sheep; life for us spelt death* for him. Life in this sense is not a heterogeneous collection of blessings; rather, they are so closely associated that John can write, 'He who has the Son has life' (1 John 5:12). By faith it begins at once. So radical is the change that existence without Christ is described as death (John 5:24, Eph. 2:1). The epithet 'eternal' has as much to do with quality as duration. The truth is, as Ryder Smith puts it, 'Apart from Christ a man is not a man. In him is life and only the living are men'.

26 **LORD:** The confession that 'Jesus is Lord' is the mark of a true Christian (1 Cor. 12:3). In the early church this was a declaration that could easily result in a grave clash with both the Jewish and Roman authorities, in the former case on a charge of blasphemy and in the latter of treason. For the Jew it was a name reserved for the one God of the Old Testament; for the Roman it was a title given to the Emperor, which the Christian could not always endorse.

To describe anyone as 'lord' implied that he carried authority. Before the ascension Jesus claimed that he had been given *all* authority in heaven and on earth – no limits here (Matt. 28:18).

But the word also implied that this was a legitimate authority. It was not seized by force but claimed by right. What God said of himself in the Old Testament, Jesus now appropriated. On two grounds God had a rightful authority over the Israelites. He was their creator (Is. 45:11–12) and their redeemer from Egyptian bondage (Ex. 20:2, 3). Because of these facts he could fairly claim their allegiance and state 'I am the Lord' (Is. 43:1). But the New Testament shows that Jesus could legitimately require the same submission. Through him the world* was created (John 1:10) and through him we were redeemed from worse bondage than that of Egypt (1 Pet. 1:18–19). This is why he could claim to be lord over the Sabbath rather than its servant (Mark 2:28). It was right for his disciples* to call him Lord, while his example showed that he was no despot and what divine Lordship really was like (John 13:13–14).

Although 'lord' was often used as a courtesy title, increasingly the ancient world ascribed it primarily to rulers and gods. Men submit to many so-called gods and lords, but for the Christian there is only one God and one Lord (1 Cor. 8:5, 6). It is against these false claims that 'Jesus is Lord' was opposed. The Emperor's authority was legitimate until it demanded divine honours. Although the authority of Jesus is universal, it is only believers who have acknowledged it. Just as Sarah gladly submitted to the lordship of Abraham in her married life (1 Pet. 3:6), so Christians gladly obey their rightful Lord. He alone is their ultimate Master. This very act of submission unites them so that they speak of 'our Lord', which also differentiates them from others.

The Lordship of Jesus was largely hidden during his earthly ministry. By the resurrection* God has made it abundantly plain, so that eventually every tongue will have to acknowledge that Jesus is Lord (Phil. 2:9, 10). This was the event that proclaimed the title. By the ascension too it is evident that Jesus shares the Father's throne and kingly rule, till the last enemy submits (Acts 2:34–6, 1 Cor. 15:28). With such a Lord daily work takes on new meaning, for we are 'serving the Lord Christ' (Col. 3:24).

36

**27  LOVE** is the very nature of God (1 John 4:8). No other word can better describe what he is like. Even grace*, which means love for the undeserving, presumes a needy situation; but God would still be love were there no need and everything perfect. The choice of the Israelites did not stem from any quality in them, but only because God loved them. His love is spontaneous and inexplicable (Deut. 7:7, 8). Furthermore, his love is not fickle. It even persists in the face of unfaithfulness and disobedience (Jer. 31:3). Supremely God demonstrated it in the gift of his Son to die for sinful men (Rom. 5:8). However much the world's sufferings may seem to cry out that God does not care, the cross ceaselessly proclaims 'God is love'.

In the ancient world love and lust became almost identical. Ritual prostitution defiled worship* in pagan cults. The New Testament writers, following the translators of the Old Testament, took up a rare word in classical Greek to convey their special meaning – *agape*. The right response to God's love was love for God and for one's fellow-men: this was how Jesus summarized the law* (Matt. 22:36–40). Love basically means caring. What then is it to love God? It involves caring about his honour, his name, his laws. This is why love and obedience are so often closely linked (Ex. 20:6). Love for God is not to be judged by intensity of feeling: the test is much more practical and more costly. 'If you love me, keep my commandments' (John 14:15). It is the prior love of Christ that takes hold of a man* and directs him into grateful service (2 Cor. 5:14–15).

To love one's neighbour involves practical care for those one encounters. The Good Samaritan did not allow racial or social reasons to impede love's prompting (Luke 10:33–4). In a nutshell the commandments of the law spelt out love (Rom. 13:10). Like a girdle, it is the quality that holds everything else in place (Col. 3:14). The description of love in 1 Cor. 13 is not mere sentiment; it contains some of the most searching statements in the Bible. It is possible to have great prophetic powers, profound knowledge*, faith*, generosity, even self-sacrifice, and yet to be love-less. This

37

*agape* is a fruit of the Spirit* (Gal. 5:22). It is the same quality of love that God bestows on his people. Hosea had to learn this lesson from his faithless wife, to continue his love for her as God maintained his love for faithless Israel (3:1). Special emphasis is laid on love for the Christian brethren, since it is a contradiction to claim to love the Father but not his children (1 John 5:1). Love needs laws to guide it, but it is not legalistic. It must sort out its own priorities, for there is no blueprint. Under the old covenant the standard was self-love (Lev. 19:18): Jesus' commandment to love was 'new' because the model was to be his own self-less love (John 13:34).

**28 MAN** is a strange mixture of light and shade, noble and despicable. Both elements are clearly expressed in the Bible (cf. Pss. 8 and 14). This apparent riddle is resolved without compromising either aspect of the truth that experience endorses.

On the one hand, Man is the pinnacle of God's creation. In the Genesis narrative, whose purpose is theological rather than scientific, the world is carefully prepared before Man is placed upon it. Everything is made ready, just as in a home before the birth of a child. Although Man has an affinity with the rest of creation (see 'Soul'), he is distinct in that he alone is made in the image of God (Gen. 1:26). This seems to imply primarily that Man is intended to act upon earth as God's representative, while at the same time he reflects the character of his Maker. God's command to multiply and to have dominion over the rest of the created order implies a positive and wholesome attitude to both sex and science (Gen. 1:28). Man and woman are complementary, being by nature incomplete when separate (Gen. 2:20–4). Despite all his privileges, he is reminded that as a creature of dust he is weak and frail (Gen. 2:7). To enjoy his position he is required to live in obedient dependence upon the God who made him.

The other side of the coin results from Man's stepping out of line and forfeiting the blessings that God intended for him. By choosing to disregard God's explicit command (Gen. 3:3), Man's relationship with God, with other people and even with the natural order, was seriously disrupted. To be driven from the Garden of Eden meant alienation from God's presence, which is the essence of spiritual death★. Human nature became contaminated (Luke 11:13). The Fourth Gospel stresses this wilful antagonism of Man against God (3:19), which culminated in the hounding of the Messiah to death on a Roman gallows. Just as at Creation he was dependent upon God, so now in his 'lostness' he cannot extricate himself but needs God to rescue him (Luke 19:10). He needs to be re-created, and this is precisely what Jesus has made possible (2 Cor. 5:17). He must first repent★ (Mark 1:15), but only the initiative of God's grace★ makes this possible.

So it is that Paul can describe a new beginning with Christ. Adam spelt death, Christ spells life★ (1 Cor. 15:22, Rom. 5:18). God's original purpose for Man becomes possible once more. Jesus Christ, the word become flesh★, *is* the image of the invisible God (Col. 1:15, John 1:14). On earth he represented his Father in perfect obedience and fully reflected the divine nature. Not only has he removed the barrier between God and Man, but this Christ now lives within every believer (Gal. 2:20) to exhibit new life. In this way God intends that each disciple should be progressively conformed to the image of his Son (Rom. 8:29). Instead of a distorted *imago Dei*, there will ultimately be a perfect resemblance.

29 **MINISTRY:** (See also 'Servant' for the wider meaning). Spiritual leadership is a necessity for the direction of the people of God. The Old Testament priesthood was God's own appointing (Num. 3:10), with the Levites as their assistants. They had the privilege of special access to God (Deut. 10:8), in

the light of which they exercised a two-fold function: Godward, to offer sacrifice*, and manward, to expound the law* (Deut. 33:10). Yet even then it was recognized that all Israel fulfilled a priestly role (Ex. 19:6). In the New Testament Jesus Christ is shown to have opened the way into the most intimate presence of God for *every* Christian to enter (Heb. 10:19–22). Consequently the whole people of God constitute a priesthood, with the dual role of offering up spiritual sacrifices and proclaiming God's saving work (1 Pet. 2:5, 9). Thus the task of the minister within the Christian church* is not that of the sacrificing priest. Some of his duties are similar, while he also incorporates certain of the functions of the prophet.

When the apostles founded a church, they appointed a group of elders to serve the community (Acts 14:23). These men were those already recognized as leaders by their seniority in secular affairs. Sometimes, in a missionary situation, a tried young man might be left in charge, such as Titus in Crete, but his objective was to appoint elders eventually (Tit. 1:5). So the Christian ministry was not hereditary: it involved a team, normally of senior men. They were to be respected for their work's sake, especially those who were teachers (1 Thess. 5:12–13, 1 Tim. 5:17). Church members were endowed with various gifts by the Spirit* for the benefit of the whole, but there was a recognized gradation of importance (1 Cor. 12:28–31). The teaching function was primary.

All these ministries were God's gift to the church (Eph. 4:11–13). Their task was to build up the people of God. Following the example of the Chief Shepherd, the elders (or under-shepherds, cf. Ezek. 34) must carry out their charge without greed or a domineering spirit (1 Pet. 5:1–3). We do not find in the New Testament a rigid pattern of ministry. For instance, 'bishops' and 'elders' were interchangeable terms (e.g. Acts 20:17, 28). The idea of a body of elders was taken over from the Jewish synagogue. For deacons there was a precedent in Hellenistic cult officials. Deacons in the Church tended to handle administrative and business affairs, but by no means exclusively. Women had their part to play also (Rom. 16:1, 2). The qualities looked for in those exercising special ministries were primarily moral and spiritual (1 Tim. 3:1–13). Paul regarded his ministry as that of a servant and a steward – Christ's 'errand-boy', responsible for feeding Christ's household with the revealed message of God's salvation*, as the words really mean (1 Cor. 4:1, 2).

The three features of this Christian ministry most needing consideration today are its teamwork, flexibility and spiritual qualifications.

30 **MIRACLE:** The ancient world was very familiar with 'wonder-workers' who caused men to marvel at their powers. Both for the Israelites and for the Christians further criteria were necessary. In Old and New Testaments there are three groups of words used for miracles, suggesting respectively wonder, power and significance. A genuinely miraculous act of God will arouse awe because it is distinctive (Jos. 3:5): it will demonstrate the power of God (Matt. 11:20): it will also be significant in revealing something about him (John 3:2). False miracles will not stand up to this threefold test, since they are deceitful, dependent on Satanic power and convey no revelation of God (2 Thess. 2:9); but their ability to delude is not underrated (Matt. 7:22–3). On all three counts the miracles of Jesus were fully attested (Acts 2:22).

Miracles must be seen within the context of divine sovereignty and providence. God is not a remote figure, occasionally intervening in the world* when affairs get out of hand. He rules over the natural order (Matt. 5:45, 6:26) and over the kingdoms of men (Dan. 4:32). Consequently there are many things that should be recognized as miracles in the widest sense (Rom. 1:20). But, in general, miracles are taken to be those events that contravene natural laws, i.e. the normal pattern of observed phenomena. Life would be impossible without these natural laws, but if

God is intimately involved in the running of his universe, they obviously impose no obligation upon him. When he acts miraculously, it is not then a haphazard intervention. Miracles in the Bible occur particularly at major moments of revelatory history, especially at the time of the Exodus and of the Incarnation. They are significant in what they indicate, not merely wonderful. This is why the New Testament invariably links one of the other categories of miracle words with that of 'wonders'. The Fourth Gospel especially concentrates on the word 'signs'. It should be noted that, even if today some scientific explanation can be given for what was then inexplicable, the fundamental idea of miracle is not altered.

The life of Jesus began with an astonishing miracle, the virgin conception, and ended with the equally remarkable sign of the resurrection*. It was only to be expected if God was to come among men in an unique way. The miracle of Jesus' sinlessness can easily be overlooked (John 8:46). He exhibited authority over nature (Mark 4:39), the ability to multiply loaves (John 6:13-14), wide powers of healing which covered many forms of disease still incurable today (e.g. Mark 9:14-27), and even authority over death* (Mark 5:35-42). Usually his healing was in response to faith* in himself, but its lack only restricted his total ministry of which healing was a part (contrast Mark 6:5, 6 with Luke 22:50-1). Human need stirred his compassion (Matt. 14:14): this was his motivation. His miracles were also an evidence of his divinity – people reacted as in the presence of God (Luke 5:26). Such power could only mean that the kingdom* of God had come (Matt. 12:28). Truly, 'nothing is too hard for the Lord'.

31 **PEACE** is a very inadequate word to express the Biblical terms it translates. For the Hebrew it involved much more than an end of hostilities or anxiety. It meant health, wholeness, harmony. A modern equivalent would be 'integration', as

opposed to every form of chaos and disruption. This can be experienced at different levels. There is the peace that conveys assurance and confidence, but it is not to be had without righteous living (Is. 32:17). For the wicked there is no such peace (Is. 57:21). The Hebrew did not make any clear distinction between an inner calm and material prosperity, so that peace may refer to physical health or affluence (Gen. 43:27, Ps. 37:11). Again, peace is to be sought in relationship to other people, though this also is the gift of God (Ps. 147:14). Such harmony is a mark of God's covenant* people. The close association of peace with salvation* underlines the fundamental need to be put in a right relationship with God to be made spiritually whole. This the Suffering Servant undertook (Is. 52:7, 53:5).

The New Testament proclaims that Christ is our peace. He has broken down the barriers that separate man* from God and man from man (Eph. 2:14-18). The old hostilities have been removed by the Cross (Col. 1:20). We stand in a new relationship both to God and to all the members of his family. A fresh harmony prevails, but it must be pursued and maintained (Rom. 12:18). It does not follow that there will be happy relations with all and sundry. On the contrary, the gospel* is divisive and may rouse bitter antagonism (Luke 12:51-3). Inward peace of mind is a fruit of the Spirit*; it is Christ's peace, which can still be experienced in the thick of suffering (Gal. 5:22, John 14:27). The one who learns to trust God and commit everything thankfully into his keeping discovers that this divine peace garrisons his heart and mind (Phil. 4:6, 7). This is the antidote to anxiety. Although the Christian, with a confident hope* of life* beyond the grave, does not need the same visible tokens of God's care in material things that the Hebrew expected, he still knows that God *does* care about every aspect of life. Modern medicine has rediscovered the close links between peace of mind and health of body*. The peace of God does indeed pass all understanding.

**32  PRAYER** is a comprehensive term for many aspects of worship*. It is an expression of filial dependence, a means of developing our personal relationship with God. Many of the problems that it arouses in our minds are at least partly resolved when we realize that in prayer we are acknowledging God's transcendent power and at the same time his active concern in human affairs. It is fundamental to prayer that we are open to God (Ps. 62:8). No attempt is to be made to hide from him what we really feel: he is great enough to take it. But unless a person is a true child of God, he has no right to expect his prayers to be answered, except for the prayer of repentance*. The Christian has been brought into a right relationship with God, so that he can meaningfully use the intimate word 'Abba', Father (Rom. 8:15, 16). Jesus' own teaching that we are to pray 'in his name' implies that only through what he has accomplished on our behalf and on his authority is access to the Father possible (John 16:23, 24).

If God is omnipotent and a God of love*, why do we need to pray at all concerning life on earth? Partly because God seeks our intimate dependence upon him; but prayer also demonstrates our care for others. That is why 'importunity', a shameless persistence, is commended (Luke 11:5–8). It is not that God is reluctant to answer, nor that there is any merit simply in the quantity of prayer. Rather we are drawn into a deep concern for the fulfilment of his loving purposes. The Bible usually speaks of God *hearing* rather than *answering* prayer, for we can never impose our will upon him. Jesus gave the supreme example of this submission in the anguish of Gethsemane (Luke 22:42). So there is nothing magical about prayer. Effectual prayer should go hand in hand with a careful observance of God's law* or it may even become an abomination (Prov. 28:9).

Christian prayers spring initially from the context of the Christian family – '*Our* Father' is the pattern. It requires an attitude of faith and expectancy (Mark 11:24). Praise and confession, petition mingled with thanksgiving (Phil. 4:6), these are the constituents of prayer. Here too provision has been made for our weakness. The Spirit*, perfectly attuned to the mind of God, prays on our behalf even when words fail us (Rom. 8:26).

**33 PREDESTINATION** has suffered from misinterpretation more than most Biblical terms. There has also been a tendency to reach 'logical' conclusions that go beyond the plain statements of the Bible, if not contradicting them. This is a truth to encourage believers, not to place limitations on evangelism or to breed despondency or even permissiveness.

Basic to the whole doctrine is the omnipotence of God. 'Is anything too hard for the Lord?' (Gen. 18:14). This mighty God so rules his universe that nothing ever gets out of control, even though it may sometimes appear so, as in the case of Job (e.g. Ps. 29:10). Therefore history is not a random series of events. God is constantly working out his purpose, even making the wrath of men to praise him. He has 'made everything for its purpose' (Prov. 16:4). The Old Testament writers, in stating this, were not in any way denying man's* freedom to act responsibly; otherwise his wrongdoing could hardly be regarded as culpable. What they sought to protect was *God's* freedom of action, whose purposes could not ultimately be frustrated. And this will of God is essentially good and merciful (Eph. 1:5, 9).

God's law* represents his will, but predestination concerns his final plan. It begins in the foreknowledge of God. Christians were chosen in Christ before the world's foundation and their names inscribed in the Lamb's book of life* (Eph. 1:4, Rev. 13:8). The whole plan of salvation* is the work of God, which ensures its fulfilment from start to finish (Rom. 8:29, 30). But again men are not just machines. God 'draws', but men have to 'come' (John 6:44). The merciful plan of God also extends beyond individuals. It comprises the wider compass of Jew and Gentile regarded as units, which Paul elaborates in Rom. 9–11. It is

important to notice that the call of Jesus in the Gospels is equivalent to an invitation and is not as precise a term as the 'elect'*
in the Epistles: Jesus distinguished between the called and the
chosen (Matt. 22:14).

The result of this doctrine, rightly understood, is to supply the
Christian with a deep confidence in the unfaltering mercy of
God and also to provide a powerful stimulus to live 'to the praise
of his glory' (Eph. 1:6, 12).


**34  RECONCILIATION:** Although this word only rarely occurs
in the New Testament, it is the term most often employed
in modern writing on the atonement. This is because it
safeguards the personal nature of God's dealings with men rather
than any impersonal transaction. Since it is a metaphor drawn
from the restoration of broken relationships, it is closely linked
with the ideas of enmity and peace*.

Reconciliation is only necessary in a situation where hostility
prevails. 'While we were enemies, we were reconciled to God',
says Paul (Rom. 5:10). Fallen man's attitude of mind is basically
antagonistic to his Creator (James 4:4). It is this which incurs
divine wrath*. So it is clear that the estrangement is caused by sin*
and that the fault lies wholly at man's door. It is man* who needs
to be reconciled and it is God alone who does it. Reconciliation
is the basic need of our disordered world, primarily of man with
God (2 Cor. 5:20), but also between men (Eph. 2:14–16) and
ultimately of the whole cosmos (Col. 1:20).

While it is plain that human sin has caused the rift and that
God is the reconciler, a personal relationship is always two-sided.
In an Egyptian papyrus of the first century A.D. an errant son
writes to his mother whom he has wronged, 'Be reconciled to
me', thus showing that the hostility must be overcome on both
sides. Inherent in the very nature of God is a hatred of sin and the
need to expunge it: his wrath is active (1 Cor. 15:25). 'Mercy and

wrath are the two ways in which God meets men. He who will not accept God's mercy stands under God's wrath' (Nygren). Thus sin creates a dual barrier to be removed – man's hostility and God's wrath. God's solution was the Cross (Rom. 5:10). Only in this way could guilt be removed, a new attitude created and God's love and honour satisfied.

When Paul states that reconciliation is *through* Christ, he is referring to the accomplished fact of the Cross (2 Cor. 5:18–21). It is not achieved merely by the inspiration of his example or some mystical experience. At the moment of history God reckoned to Christ's account what previously was held against us (vv. 18 and 21). Moreover, it is important to see that this is not a case of a loving Saviour appeasing an angry Father. This is a travesty of the truth: '*God* was in Christ'. Nor does this imply an automatic restoration of all men, for Christians have a ministry of urging men to be reconciled to God (vv. 18 and 20). Reconciliation is a gift that Christ purchased by his death; our responsibility is to receive it and make it our own (Rom. 5:11). Everyone who does so is then *in* Christ and a new creation has taken place (2 Cor. 5:17). Not only is the past record blotted out, but the love of God poured into our hearts by the Holy Spirit transforms our attitude and the new relationship becomes a vital experience (Rom. 5:5).

35 **REDEMPTION** means strictly a purchasing *back* by the original owner. While theologically correct, it is not the precise significance of the Hebrew and Greek words which rather emphasize a costly deliverance. 'Ransom' is therefore a better translation. In the social and religious life of Israel the idea occurs frequently and sets the stage for its specific use in relation to the atonement won by Christ. The difficulty is to know how far the metaphor can be taken: its danger can be seen in the way the

Cappadocian Fathers tried to answer the question, 'To whom was the ransom-price paid?'

In Hebrew there are three terms used, each with a slightly different shade of meaning. *Padah* is the straightforward word for commercial transactions. When the Levites are appointed to replace the first-born males, the 273 first-born in excess are to be ransomed at 5 shekels apiece (Num. 3:40-51). In order to retain the first-born, something must be given in their place. A man cannot ransom his own life because it is too costly (Ps. 49:7-9): the initiative must lie with God. *Ga'al* originates in family law. It means to 'play the part of a kinsman', whether as an avenger of blood or in marrying the widow of a near relative. Boaz fulfilled the latter duty for Ruth, which also involved financial cost (Ruth 3:13, 4:3, 4). When this term is used of God, as in the latter part of Isaiah, it also emphasizes the relationship in which God stands to his people (e. g. Is. 43:1). *Kopher*, a root with several meanings, implies a ransom-price that results in deliverance (Ex. 30:12). 'The idea common to these three forms of redemption is that of substitution; man gives something in order to receive another thing in its place' (E. Jacob). When God is redeemer, it is *God* who gives something.

Against this background Christian redemption takes shape. Man finds himself a slave – to sin★ (John 8:34), to false gods (Gal. 4:8), even to the Law★ (Gal. 4 and 5). A price must be paid for his release, identified as 'the precious blood★ of Christ' (1 Pet. 1:18, 19). What man could not do for himself, Christ did on his behalf. It was a transaction of incalculable cost. For the redeemed the one who purchased them is their new owner, their bodies are his property (1 Cor. 6:19, 20), but the final redemption of the body lies in the future (Rom. 8:23). The idea of a substitutionary equivalent for ransoming men is found in the teaching of Jesus himself (Mark 10:45).

It has been argued that, when Paul and John spoke of 'ransom' they had in mind the contemporary method for release or 'manumission' of slaves. 'The owner comes with the slave to the temple, sells him there to the god, and receives the purchase money from the temple treasury, the slave having previously paid it in there out of his savings. The slave is now the property of the god: not, however, a slave of the temple, but a protégé of the god. Against all the world, especially his former master, he is a completely free man' (A. Deissmann). Though the parallels are striking, the Old Testament scriptures are the predominant influence.

**36  REGENERATION:** So radical is the change that God effects in a believer that it can be defined in terms of a new creation (2 Cor. 5:17), resurrection* (Col. 2:12) and a new birth (John 3:6,7). All these metaphors emphasize God's initiative and a profound change. Ezekiel forecast national renewal (37:5, 6, 36:26) and the Psalmist an individual inner transformation (51:10), but the idea of a new birth is only explicit in the New Testament. Here there are three distinct emphases.

First, the Fourth Gospel stresses the actual event. For someone to see the Kingdom* of God, let alone enter it, he must be born again (3:3, 5). This new birth is not dependent upon man, but comes from God and his Spirit* (1:13, 3:6). The Greek word here for 'again' can also be translated 'from above' and may be a deliberate ambiguity, since both meanings fit the context. When Jesus included 'of water' (3:5), he may have alluded to the idea of cleansing in Ezekiel or to John's baptism of repentance* or to an anticipation of Christian baptism*. This last interpretation fits the character of John's Gospel and ties in with the probable significance of the 'washing of regeneration' in Tit. 3:5. It is also clear that this new birth takes place in response to the Word of God (James 1:18, 1 Pet. 1:23).

Whereas in John 1 and 3 the aorist tense is mainly used, in 1 John it is always the perfect: the use of perfects indicates that

49

this single, initial act carries with it far-reaching results. So this epistle stresses the ensuing characteristics of the regenerate man. The first mark is righteousness* (2:29), behaviour in conformity with God's will. This will include the avoidance of sin*, because his new nature makes a life of sin utterly incongruous (3:9). John clearly does not mean by this a sinless perfection, for he has already exposed any such claims (1:8); rather, he is pointing to a new character and habit. This new birth detaches a man from the world* and attaches him to God. The world's pressures will no longer prevail over him (5:4). The second mark is a love* for Christian brethren where there is now a new, spiritual family-tie: moreover, God's nature of love must show itself in his children (4:7). Thirdly, there will follow a faith* in Jesus Christ which will persist (5:1). John is saying, in effect, that when these marks are not evident, there is no regeneration. Obedience, love and faith are the only certain signs.

Finally, there is a stress on the consummation of this new life*, for Christians possess a living hope* (1 Pet. 1:3). The whole life of believers is now being refashioned: then the transformation will be complete. The same word-root in Matt. 19:28 (translated 'new world') suggests that the full effects will be on a cosmic scale. See also Rom. 8:20-4.

37 **REPENTANCE:** The first recorded preaching of Jesus contains the call to repent (Mark 1:14-15). The Greek word means literally 'to have second thoughts', 'to change one's mind', but in the New Testament it is always strongly coloured by the Hebrew idea, which is 'to turn'. The two themes are brought together specifically in Acts 3:19 and 26:20. This makes it plain that repentance is never mere emotional regret for the past. It is possible to be deeply ashamed of one's conduct without ever turning wholeheartedly from it. Such was the case with Judas (Matt. 27:3-5), so completely different from that of Simon

Peter. There is a 'worldly grief' that is nothing more than hurt pride: a 'godly sorrow' produces genuine repentance (2 Cor. 7:9–10). This begins negatively with an admission of guilt and error: it proceeds positively with a forsaking of sin* and turning to God – thus an essential companion to faith*. Repentance may be summed up as a change of attitude leading to a change of direction.

It would be quite wrong to play down the importance of this hatred of sin and grief over the past, since repentance is to lead men to salvation*, which involves deliverance from sin's clutches. This loathing is forcefully expressed in the penitential psalms, such as 32 and 51. A recognition of the real significance of sin, an affront to God himself (Ps. 51:4), must inevitably produce such a reaction. It only becomes morbid and unhealthy when the guilt remains unconfessed or when God's promise of pardon is not trusted.

Repentance and faith are the basic conditions that God has laid down for salvation. It is unthinkable that we should expect forgiveness from God without any intention of forsaking those very sins that need to be pardoned. Thus John the Baptist linked repentance and forgiveness (Mark 1:4): the risen Christ charged his followers to do the same in their preaching (Luke 24:47). John had made it clear that this was no mere formula of words. A new pattern of life would be the proof of its genuineness (Matt. 3:8), just as James in his epistle set up a similar test for faith. But although all this involves responsible action on our part, it does not alter the fact that salvation is wholly God's doing, for which we can take no credit to ourselves whatever. The opportunity to repent is God's gift (Acts 11:18, 2 Tim. 2:25). Through divine initiative the kingdom* of God draws near and prompts penitence (Matt. 3:2). God is ever sending his messengers (Matt. 4:17, Rom. 10:14–15). His constant acts of kindness ought to elicit such a response (Rom. 2:4). Moreover, this is no light option. God has shown infinite patience towards men's heedlessness: now he *commands* all men everywhere to repent (Acts 17:30).

Nor are lukewarm Christians excluded from the charge (Rev. 3:19).

When the Old Testament speaks of God repenting, it implies a change in his relations with men. Clearly this must be different from man's repentance, since 'he is not a man, that he should repent' (1 Sam. 15:29). In fact an entirely different word is used.

**38  RESURRECTION:** From the moment that Jesus began to teach explicitly that he would be put to death, he always added that he would also be raised again (Matt. 16:21). His death and resurrection were indissolubly bound together. Three times he had himself brought back people from the dead. In the case of Lazarus, Jesus explained to Martha that he himself was the resurrection and the life* and, by his explanation of what this meant, he showed that it involved much more than physical resuscitation (John 11:24-6). The resurrection was an integral part of his saving work.

Less than two months after the crucifixion, the disciples were boldly asserting the resurrection (Acts 2:24-32). They proclaimed that *God* had raised Jesus, thus vindicating the claims of his Son and setting the seal of divine approval upon his work. It was no random event but had been forecast in the Old Testament as part of God's saving purpose. The appearances to the disciples of their risen Lord*, of which the New Testament records ten separate instances, constituted overwhelming proof (Acts 1:3). The empty tomb, the disciples' new-found courage, the inability of the authorities to refute the Christian claims, the choice of the first day of the week for the breaking of bread (recalling Luke 24:35) – all these point to the fact of the resurrection.

But the New Testament is not concerned with adducing evidence so much as explaining the theological significance of what had occurred. With regard to the *past*, this was the conclusive sign that the man Jesus was God's Son in an unique sense

(Rom. 1:4). Our justification★ was thereby ensured (Rom. 4:25), for if Jesus Christ had not been raised there would be no guarantee that he had effectively atoned for our sins★ (1 Cor. 15:17); Christian faith★ would be empty and presumptuous. Instead, the devil★ and death★ had been conquered (Heb. 2:14–15). As for the *present*, the believer is so united with Christ that he shares in both the benefits of his death and the power of his resurrection (Phil. 3:10). This experience is symbolized by the descent into and emergence from the water of baptism★ (Rom. 6:3, 4). It is not just pictorial language. Because we have already risen with Christ to this new life, we are to aim at that which befits it (Col. 3:1).

But the resurrection of Jesus touches our *future* also. Eventually this new life will affect the body★ of the believer as well as his spirit★, of which Jesus' healing ministry was a foretaste. The connecting link is the working of the Holy Spirit within us, both now and at the final resurrection (Rom. 8:11). The raising of Jesus was like the first sheaf of the harvest, the assurance of all that is to follow (1 Cor. 15:23). Our bodies will then be transformed to resemble his resurrection body (1 Cor. 15:51–6, Phil. 3:21): the dead will be raised, the living will be changed. This new body is both *from below* (somehow linked with our former earthly body) and also *from above* (newly prepared by God, 2 Cor 5:1–3). Paul seems here to imply that those who die before Christ's return will be in a disembodied, unnatural state, though with Christ (Phil. 1:23), until the resurrection. Then the whole man★, body and spirit, will enjoy the fulness of Christ's resurrection life.

39 **RIGHTEOUSNESS** is God's requirement of man★. It involves behaviour that conforms to God's will as revealed in his law★.

A religion without it is loathsome to God (Amos 5:24), but he loves righteous deeds because he himself is righteous (Ps. 11:7). This does not mean that God stands under some moral law of righteousness, for he himself is its source. Because he is the judge of all the earth, he is concerned to promote it. Therefore the righteousness of God is often associated with God's acts of deliverance, since man in his weakness needs divine help and intervention (Ps. 71:14–16). Somehow he must obtain such a share in God's righteousness that his life* will be acceptable with God.

The death* of Christ is the supreme saving act of God that reveals God's righteousness. This is the essence of the gospel* (Rom. 1:16, 17). Two courses lie open to man – either to establish a righteousness of his own or to accept by faith* the gift of God's righteousness (Phil. 3:9). For the most part the Jews persisted on the former course. Their misplaced zeal was doomed to failure, for they did not understand the true function of the law: 'no human being will be justified in his sight by works of the law' (Rom. 10:1–10, 3:20). The new thing that Christ has done is to make it possible for sinful men to be pardoned and accepted by God and then enabled to live a righteous life. It necessitated both a life of righteousness that was always perfectly attuned to the Father's will and also his atoning death that fully met the righteous demands of God's broken law (Rom. 3:25, 26). Through God's initiative men can now be placed in a right relationship with him. God's righteousness offers justification* as a free gift (Rom. 5:17). This legal sense of righteousness is only half the truth. At the same time that God justifies, he also bestows a new life by regeneration* in the Spirit*. The Christian now has within him the life-principle of the righteous God. The child will display the character of the parent in right conduct (1 John 2:29).

The whole Biblical message is summarized in this word 'righteousness'. The character of God is such that he ever seeks to ensure it prevails. In the coming of Christ it was uniquely displayed. Now Christians enjoy a standing of complete acceptance with God: they are 'legally' righteous. Progressively by the Spirit they are now enabled to be 'morally' righteous. These two lines converge and will meet in God himself at the end of the age, for *he* is our righteousness.

**40  SACRIFICE** involves a gift, but its significance may vary considerably. Pagans would practise it to bribe their gods, but the Israelite system was emphatically God-given, which alone ensured its efficacy (Lev. 17:11). Carried out from the earliest times, it was reorganized under the Mosaic law★. There were special blood★ sacrifices for *entering* into a covenant★ relationship with God (Gen. 15, Ex. 24) and thereafter for *living* within the covenant community (Lev. 1–7). The latter had 'a threefold function: it was an expression of gratitude, it aimed at communion with God, and it was designed to bring about expiation of sin' (H. Ringgren). Nevertheless the limitations of the sacrificial system were all too evident. The repetition on each Day of Atonement indicated its incompleteness. Access into the Holy of Holies remained barred. Instead of providing a remedy, it renewed a consciousness of sin★. And how could a mere animal's blood atone? (Heb. 10:1–4). Moreover, the Israelite sacrifices dealt only with sins of ignorance or carelessness, never with acts of wilful disobedience.

Christ's atoning work is often described in sacrificial terms that recall the Old Testament. He is the paschal lamb, who had to be without blemish to be acceptable (1 Cor. 5:7, 1 Pet. 1:18, 19). As both High Priest and victim he secured an eternal redemption★ and opened the way into God's presence for every believer to follow (Heb. 9:11, 12). This once-for-all sacrifice requires no repetition. It was only in anticipation of this that God could accept men through the animal sacrifices under the old covenant (Heb. 9:15). Consequently, Christ has fulfilled the Old Testament sacrificial system, now to be discarded (Heb. 10:5–10). Christians are enabled in a new way to make acceptable offerings to God as his covenant people because their conscience★ has been purified (Heb. 9:13). The spirit-filled man now offers *spiritual* sacrifices (1 Pet. 2:5). Supremely, this means the yielding of ourselves to God's service. If Jesus surrendered his body★, how much more should we (Rom. 12:1, 2). This is the greatest token of gratitude that we can render. Praise and thanksgiving, a good and generous life – these are the sacrifices that God seeks and which glorify him (Heb. 13:15, 16). Even faith* is an offering to God (Phil. 2:17). Christ, our High Priest, alone provided the sacrifice that atones for sin; the other elements of the role of priest devolve upon the whole Christian community. The priesthood of all believers eliminates a priestly caste.

41 **SAINT:** Popular usage has restricted this word to a select minority of outstandingly godly people, but the New Testament applies it to all Christians. Paul could so address the Corinthian church*, whose moral conduct left much to be desired (1 Cor. 1:2). The explanation lies partly in the meaning of the word-group when applied to God himself. So transcendent is he that men must stand in awe of him. To have seen God filled Manoah with fear for his life (Judg. 13:22). But the startling paradox is that this holy God who is a consuming fire (Heb. 12:29) calls men to share in his holiness (1 Pet. 1:15, 16). Sanctity means separateness. God is uniquely set apart from all creation, but through the cross of Christ a way into the presence of God (symbolized by the most holy place in the tabernacle) has been opened for us (Heb. 10:19–22). The unapproachable God has made himself approachable through Christ.

Christians are called to be holy like the one who called them. Redemption* always carries this requirement (Num. 15:40, 41). It involves both a separation from all that is sinful and complete dedication to God, so that holiness is by no means purely negative. Nor is it a cold asceticism. Creation is to be enjoyed by the child of God unselfishly and thankfully (1 Tim. 4:4, 5). The saints of God in their turn respect God's holiness by hallowing his name and reverencing Christ as Lord in their hearts, for sanctity is basically an internal quality (1 Pet. 3:15).

There is a sense in which sanctification is the status of every child of God and therefore complete and final, because Christ is our sanctification (1 Cor. 1:30). Christians have been set apart once and for all as God's people. Far more frequently in the New Testament, however, sanctification is described as a process of growth, where one saint differs from another, in contrast with justification* where all stand on an equal footing. No man can live a holy life unaided, but the Spirit* has been given to enable us to live according to God's requirements (Rom. 8:3, 4). The inner clash of the flesh* and the Spirit will always be with us in this life. A victorious faith* is not a passive reliance but stimulates a personal discipline of both body and mind (1 Cor. 9:27, Phil. 4:8). This progress in sanctity will continue till we see the Lord face to face, when our spiritual state will correspond with our status as God's saints.

42  **SALVATION** is a far more comprehensive term than is usually recognized. The Romans gave the emperor Augustus the title 'Saviour of the World', but neither emperor-worship nor the mystery-cults proved effective or satisfying. When the angel instructed Joseph to name Mary's child 'Jesus', meaning 'Saviour', a new dimension was given to the word (Matt. 1:21); but already the Old Testament had indicated something of what this would imply.

Salvation means deliverance from a situation out of which man* cannot rescue himself. This is why ultimately God is the Saviour, because he is omnipotent (Is. 43:10, 11). For the Israelite, God's deliverance was by no means confined to the 'spiritual' sphere: far more frequently it was from physical misfortune – drought, famine, sickness, slavery in Egypt or exile in Babylon. Salvation concerns the whole man and, therefore, touches every department of life*. No event was so influential upon Israelite thinking as the Exodus, so much so that it was recalled at each of the three great annual religious festivals. This was a deliverance from physical enemies, but the result would be dedicated service for God, as the introduction to the ten commandments make plain (Ex. 20:2). Moses and Elijah on the Transfiguration Mount significantly described Jesus' impending death* also as an 'exodus' (Luke 9:30, 31). These great salvation events originate in the grace* of God (Deut. 7:7, 8): they result in a covenant* community, for salvation is not merely individualistic (Ex. 19: 4–6): and sacrifice* is the means of its accomplishment (Ex. 12:13).

The early Christians were certain that they lived in 'the last days'. Salvation was a present possession, yet its future consummation was also awaited (Tit. 2:11, 13). The Christian lives between the completed work of salvation by Christ, the historic events of the Incarnation, Atonement and Resurrection*, and the final subjugation of every enemy beneath his feet (1 Cor. 15:24, 25). He can confidently assert that he *has* been saved (Eph. 2:5), for the victory of the Cross ensures pardon and release from sin's* domination. It enables him to face the future with equanimity, because he knows that he is now accepted in Christ and has already passed from death to life (John 5:24). This is wholly God's doing, appropriated by faith*. But the Christian also foresees the time when he *will* be saved from the very presence of sin and the downward pull of the flesh*. He eagerly anticipates seeing his Lord* face to face and being changed into his likeness, with a transformed body* that will be the perfect vehicle for expressing a transformed character (1 Cor. 15:54). This will be perfection for the Christian community as well as for the individual. In the meantime, a foretaste of this consummation is given through the Spirit*, whereby we are empowered against sin and progressively sanctified (Rom. 8:4, 23). Past, present and future – these are the three tenses of salvation.


43 **SERVANT:** Service should be one of the most distinctive marks of the Christian church*. It is an ideal derived from Christ himself. The occasion when he washed the disciples'* feet in the upper room must have left an indelible impression upon

those who only a little earlier had been jostling for positions of authority. 'I have given you an example' (John 13:14, 15).

Behind the ministry of Jesus lies the pattern of the Servant Songs in Isaiah (42:1-4, 49:1-6, 50:4-7, 52:13-53:12). Two themes predominate – obedience and suffering. Mankind was created to be the servant of the Lord*. Disobedience narrowed the field down, first to the nation of Israel, then to the godly remnant within the nation, finally to the Suffering Servant whose role was fulfilled by Jesus Christ. The people would be restored by him to a covenant* relationship with God (42:6), of which the Lord's Supper is a memorial. The Servant represents the people: so Jesus underwent John's baptism* of repentance* and finally died vicariously to ransom men for God (Mark 10:45). When John described him as 'the Lamb of God', he probably was referring to the Suffering Servant, since the same word in Aramaic (the common language of the day) meant either 'lamb' or 'servant' (John 1:29, cf. Is. 53:7). Jesus specifically cited this passage as being fulfilled by himself (Luke 22:37). In perfect obedience to his Father, he suffered on our behalf in order to bring us back to God.

This unique service of Christ was not intended to stop there. The servant church is to continue this ministry*. What had narrowed down to the One is now to expand in the many. Ransomed men are doubly conscious of their allegiance. So Paul delighted to call himself the bond-slave of Christ, a willing and obedient servant (Rom. 1:1). He knew himself to be set apart to preach the gospel* and so help restore men to a right relationship with God. Such service would necessitate suffering, not to atone for sin because that was the unique work of Christ, but because of the reception that the faithful witness inevitably receives (Col. 1:24). The same word for ministry is used to describe both prayer* and preaching as well as supplying food to the needy (Acts 6:1, 4), so that Christian service does not separate the sacred and the secular. Special officers within the Church are appointed to serve the flock and not lord it over them (1 Pet. 5:2, 3). So fundamental is this spirit of service that Jesus said, 'He who is greatest among you shall be your servant' (Matt. 23:11).

44 **SIN:** The philosophical problem of the origin of sin does not concern the Biblical writers. Sin entered the world through the Devil*, who 'sinned from the beginning' (1 John 3:8), that is from the moment he fell. All human sin is ultimately attributable to him, but this in no way diminishes Man's* responsibility for his behaviour. In the account of the Fall the attempts by Adam and Eve to transfer the responsibility for their disobedience elsewhere are fruitless. What a man sows, he must also reap (Gal. 6:7).

Since the main theme of the Bible is salvation*, it is imperative to understand the nature of the sin from which Man needs to be saved. The clearest definition is in 1 John 3:4, 'Sin is lawlessness'. This does not mean being without a moral law, but the deliberate violation of the law* of God. Sin is rebellion. Paul equates sin with being the enemies of God (Rom. 5:8, 10). The range of Hebrew and Greek words for sin is very extensive, with the ideas of missing the mark, overstepping the line, erring and ignorance of what should have been known. In both languages the commonest terms employed mean 'missing the mark', indicating that sins of omission are just as serious as those of commission (Rom. 3:23). The worst sins are the deliberate reversing of moral values (the sin against the Holy Spirit, Matt. 12:31) and the rejection of Christ's offer of salvation (Heb. 2:3): so long as a man persists in either of them he places himself outside the benefits of God's grace*. Since God's law is concerned not only with man's relationship to God, but also with his association with his fellow men, there is no real distinction between religious and other sins. All are an offence against God. David recognized this after his adultery with Bathsheba, if Ps. 51:4 is correctly linked with that occasion.

Ps. 19:12-14 graphically portrays the stages of sin's development. First, there are secret faults (the law made special allowance for them, Lev. 4): then presumptuous sins, that bubble over suddenly and can easily get dominion over us: finally there is wilful rebellion against the Lord. The wages of sin is death*, both physical and spiritual (Rom. 6:23). Even to break the law at only one point is to be guilty of all, for the law is an entity in itself (James 2:10). Moreover, because no man lives to himself, what may appear as an individual matter has severe effects upon others. Achan never imagined that his theft would cause such havoc and destruction (Josh. 7:5, 24). But sin, like its source, is ever deceitful: it blinds and it hardens (Heb. 3:13).

Sin is universal and therefore all men are guilty before God (Rom. 3:9-20). Since Adam men have inherited a bias toward sin (Ps. 51:5). But Paul goes further in speaking of this solidarity of mankind. Through Adam condemnation and death came upon all men (Rom. 5:18, 12). Just as sin is not treated lightly, so its removal is a costly matter. (See also 'Flesh', 'Temptation'.)

45 **SOUL:** The Hebrew concept of man*, so very different from later Greek ideas, makes it exceedingly difficult to translate the word *nephesh*. Our popular use of 'soul' is very alien to what they believed. The same word is used for man becoming a living *being* and for every living *creature* (Gen. 2:7, 19). Human affinity with the animal order could not be more vividly expressed, but man is distinct in the manner God breathed into his nostrils the breath of life*. This implied affinity with God also, in whose image he was created, explains the heinousness of any human sexual relations with animals (Ex. 22:19). Since Gen. 2 twice spoke of *living* souls, it is not so surprising to find *nephesh* used for a corpse in Lev. 21:1. From this we can deduce that for the Hebrews a soul implied the whole of a man's being, not an internal portion locked in the body*. If different organs of the

61

body express personality from one aspect (e.g. the bowels suggest compassion), the soul is all-inclusive and not restricted to the internal side of a man's life. An approximate psychological equation is that a living soul equals flesh★ animated by the divine breath or Spirit★. When the Psalmist cries, 'Bless the Lord, O my soul' (Ps. 103:1, 2), he is appealing to his entire personality. Thus frequently in the Old Testament the writers speak of 'souls' when we would simply say 'people' (e.g. Ex. 1:5).

Since the Greek language had no precise equivalent to *nephesh*, the New Testament authors had to employ the term *psyche* as the most comparable word. Nevertheless their conception of man remained thoroughly Jewish. Mary's Magnificat, so steeped in Old Testament devotion, begins in a typically Hebrew style, 'My soul magnifies the Lord' (Luke 1:46). Just as Mary can speak of herself in this manner, so also people are called 'souls' (Acts 2:41, Rom. 13:1). Here the linguistic similarity ends, for *psyche* is used to describe both physical life on the one hand (Matt. 16:25, Luke 12:20) and the inner life of the spirit on the other (Matt. 10:28). The context determines the meaning. But this is still very far from the Greek idea of an immortal soul entombed in the body. Even where *psyche* is roughly equivalent to a man's spirit, there is no suggestion of innate immortality. Immortality is the prerogative of God alone (1 Tim. 6:15-16), though he graciously imparts a share in it to believers. Christianity is not concerned with the survival of the spirit alone but with the resurrection★ of the body, the whole man and not a part.

**46 SPIRIT:** Breath, wind and spirit can all be denoted by the same word. When used of God it implies his irresistible power. Hence the contrast with the weakness of the flesh★ (Is. 31:3). Whether it be in the creation of matter (Ps. 33:6) or physical life (Gen. 2:7) or in the bestowal of talent (Ex. 31:3-5), God is personally active and accomplishes what he chooses. Being the activity of God, the Spirit's work is always moral; only by the Spirit of the Lord* has the prophet the authority to denounce evil (Mic. 3:8). While the working of the Spirit is primarily creative and life-giving, at the same time it passes human comprehension, like the wind. Consequently the experience of being 'born of the Spirit' cannot be measured or judged by the world* (John 3:8). See also 'Regeneration'.

Whereas one might conclude from the Old Testament that the Spirit was an impersonal force, the close links between Jesus and the Spirit prove decisively that the Spirit is a Person. The work of Christ and the work of the Spirit are inextricably bound together. The promised Comforter is Jesus' other self and yet distinct (John 14:18, 26). It could not be more clearly expressed than in the command of Jesus to baptize in the *one* name of Father, Son and Holy Spirit (Matt. 28:19). As foretold in Joel 2:28-29, there would be an outpouring of the Spirit in the last days on an entirely new scale. After the limitations of Jesus' life in the flesh, the risen Lord brought into existence the age of the Spirit, the age of power, which makes its impact on all believers (Rom. 1:3, 4). Pentecost inaugurated this new era.

Since the Spirit is concerned with the gift of life*, both physical and spiritual, the Biblical writers can speak both of man's spirit and God's Spirit. Every living person possesses the former, but only the Christian possesses the latter (Rom. 8:9). It is this that unites the Christian community and transforms isolated individuals into living members of the body* of Christ (Eph. 4:4). The Spirit reproduces the character of the parent in the child, of God in the Christian. He prompts the intimate cry 'Abba, Father'; he provides the inner conviction that we are indeed children of God; he intercedes for us when words fail (Rom. 8:15-16, 26). God's people also worship* in a distinctive way. This is not simply an activity of man's spirit, but also the work of the Spirit of God, who permeates and directs their worship (Phil. 3:3). The special functions and endowments of the members of the church are apportioned by the Spirit (1 Cor. 12:7-11),

63

'for the common good'. He also supplies the authority and power for effective witness (Acts 1:8).

The working out in the Christian's life of all the benefits procured by Christ is the Spirit's task on our behalf. Always he glorifies Christ, focusing attention upon him (John 16:14). No wonder that Paul urges his readers to go on being filled with the Spirit.

**47 TEMPTATION** in old English meant 'testing', without necessarily implying any incitement to sin★. It is in this unrestricted sense that the Bible uses it. God tests men to determine the quality of their profound allegiance (Ex. 20:20). Abraham demonstrated his loyalty in such a situation (Gen. 22:1). Indeed, man★ would be morally and spiritually weak and immature without such testing, but he is blessed if he endures it (James 1:12). Every occasion of trial provides the opportunity to make a step either forward or backward. While God desires the former and therefore allows the testing to take place, the Devil★ seeks to induce a retrograde step away from God's will. This is most clearly seen in the temptation of Jesus, when he was led into the wilderness by the *Spirit*★ to be tempted by the *Devil* (Matt. 4:1). God cannot tempt men in the way that Satan does, as it would conflict with his nature (James 1:13).

Now Jesus Christ was tempted in every respect as we are, but he never sinned (Heb. 4:15). Besides being an encouragement to the Christian, this confirms the fact that temptation is not sin. God is always in control of the situation, ensuring that there is a way of escape (1 Cor. 10:13). When we do succumb to temptation, we are without excuse. The heartening feature in times of trial is that God limits Satan's devices in order to bring good out of his evil intentions. Such was the case with Job, where Satan is twice told, 'Thus far and no farther' (1:12, 2:6). Temptation leads to sin when its suggestion is welcomed in our thoughts.

So James graphically portrays this 'life-cycle' of sin, from the moment desire enters (1:14–15). The battle-ground is the mind (2 Cor. 10:5).

Satan ever seeks to get an advantage over the Christian, so we ought not to be ignorant of his devices (2 Cor. 2:11). The test may come in a direct frontal assault when he attacks as a roaring lion (1 Pet. 5:8), or it may be cunning and insidious when he approaches as an angel of light (2 Cor. 11:14–15). That is why the Lord's Prayer contains the petition, 'Lead us not into temptation'. It is not a cowardly request for an easy path, but an urgent plea for protection out of awareness of our weakness. To try to put God to the test is forbidden because it is totally unwarranted (Ex. 17:7), since he has given ample testimony to his dependability. But there is a right place for testing ourselves (2 Cor. 13:5). It will better enable the Christian to oppose Satan's advances. He will never forget that the Devil's authority was smashed at the Cross (John 12:31). He will not take unnecessary risks that give the tempter a foothold (Eph. 4:27). He will resist every assault, knowing his own trials are not unique, but he will trust wholly in the Stronger than the strong for victory (1 Pet. 5:9).

48 **WORLD:** Through the Word was the world created (John 1:10). The Greek *kosmos* means strictly 'the ordered world', which aptly describes the work of creation which God saw to be good. But the entry of sin\* has left it sadly *dis*ordered (Rom. 5:12). Every aspect was affected, but the prime evidence is man\*. So *kosmos* frequently describes mankind in his fallen state. Since the Devil\* has usurped God's rightful rule over men, he is called 'the prince of this world' (John 14:30). The whole world lies in his power (1 John 5:19). Inevitably men suffer in consequence. They are plunged in a Satanic darkness, where only the light of Christ offers any relief (John 8:12). But the coming of

65

Christ leads to judgment*, for the world must make a choice. By crucifying him the world passed judgment on itself, though this did not spell final condemnation for all (John 12:31-2).

This condition of mankind has resulted in a whole attitude of mind that rejects the authority of God. Men without Christ live in a society that revolves around a different axis. 'World' is used to describe this system of thought which is hostile to God (James 4:4). The follower of Christ will not be surprised when he encounters the world's hatred, because this was how his Lord was treated (John 15:18-19). It is the spirit of antichrist (1 John 4:3). Now Christ came to save the world. The gift of the Spirit* can deliver men from the bondage of the world's spirit (1 Cor. 2:12). No one can achieve this by himself, but through God's gift of new life* received through faith* victory is possible. More than that, victory is certain because Christ himself overcame the world and it is into the fruits of his victory that we may enter. This does not mean that the Christian must withdraw into monastic seclusion; Jesus specifically prayed that his disciples should not be isolated from the world but kept from the wiles of its prince (John 17:25). The Christian is no longer *of* the world, allied to this fallen society, for its characteristics, such as pride and lust, are alien to him now (1 John 2:16). But he must still live *in* it, while avoiding the contamination of its outlook.

It is important to notice that this Christian attitude to the world is not contempt. God loved it and sent his Son to save it (John 3:16). The individuals that constitute it matter to God, even though its corrupt manner of life is repudiated. The material things of God's creation are also not to be despised, even if affected by the fall, since God has a future for them also (Rom. 8:21).

**49  WORSHIP:** One word in Hebrew denotes work, service and worship. It is a necessary reminder that all worship is an expression of service to God. Nor is this service confined to the sanctuary, but it should pervade all work outside. Yet activity alone is no substitute for coming humbly into the presence of God. Our English word means to acknowledge someone's worth, which is the invitation of the Psalmist: 'Ascribe to the Lord the glory due to his name' (96:8). While we may worship God individually, he summons his people *together* for worship. The servants* of the Lord* are not intended to live in isolation. By meeting in the same place (Acts 2:44) they are enabled to get their lives in true perspective and to give mutual encouragement (Heb. 10:24–5).

To acknowledge God's worth means that worship is a response on man's part. Without a prior revelation, we would not know how to worship. Thus the Psalms of praise elaborate both who God is and what he has done. For instance, Ps. 29 tells of his sovereignty as King and 106 describes his mercy despite the wilful disobedience of the Israelites. This explains the important place given to the reading of Scripture in both Jewish synagogue and Christian church. Without it, worship quickly becomes misdirected or contentless. Of course, personal experience of God's goodness adds further ground for response (e.g. Ps. 116), but the reading and exposition of God's word is primary.

In speaking to the woman of Samaria Jesus clearly linked understanding of what we are doing with worship in Spirit* (John 4:22–4). Unless our worship corresponds to the truth about God, it will be unacceptable. But God is spirit and therefore worship must be spiritual. Empty forms are useless and against such the prophets inveighed (Mic. 6:6–8). This does not mean that all outward actions and set liturgical forms should be abolished. Jesus himself provided the pattern of the Lord's Prayer and the early Christians soon produced credal statements. At the same time, there was permitted a much greater freedom of the Spirit* for congregational participation than is customary today, with the proviso that it was edifying and orderly (1 Cor. 14:26, 40).

The usual place for meeting was a home (e.g. Col. 4:15). Our special buildings obscure the advantages of the house-church, for here it is more apparent that worship is closely associated with everyday life and there is greater scope for spontaneity. Besides the reading and preaching, there would be prayer* and praise in the context of informal fellowship*. Singing too is a natural way of giving thanks (Col. 3:16). So far as was practicable, the early Christians met on the Lord's Day, a constant reminder of the risen Christ in their midst. Worship had its practical expression in the giving of an offertory (1 Cor. 16:1, 2). The reminder of God's mercies inspires fresh dedication and should send the worshipper back into the world* refreshed for service (Rom. 12:1, 2).

50 **WRATH:** With the wrath of man we are familiar enough, but when this is ascribed to God, it is easily misconstrued. To speak of the God of wrath of the Old Testament and the God of love* of the New is totally misleading. In each Testament both attributes are frequently applied to God. It requires a lot of special pleading to reduce this wrath to the *impersonal* law of cause and effect when there is persistence in sin*, as C. H. Dodd argued in his commentary on Rom. 1:18. Rather, it is the unswerving *attitude* of God towards sin. The Bible uses human terms, but divine wrath transcends human wrath just as divine love transcends human love. It is neither passionate nor irrational and it is not in conflict with God's love. While it is clear that love is the essential nature of God (1 John 4:8) so that, in the ideal situation, there would be no place for wrath, yet it is still true as Lactantius said in the third century, 'He who does not hate does not love'. Divine wrath, like judgment*, has an ultimately constructive role, to purge out all dross.

68

The special privileges accorded the Israelites included possession of the law*. By its incisive definition of offences so as to
dispel ignorance, it can even be said to 'bring wrath' (Rom.
4:15). By very nature all of us incur it (Eph. 2:3), yet 'Christ
redeemed us from the curse of the law, having become a curse for
us' (Gal. 3:13). Consequently this wrath of God must always be
seen in close association with God's *patience* and mercy. God's
covenant* love held back the full expression of his wrath, though
wickedness sometimes reached such a peak that it momentarily
brimmed over (Is. 54:8, 10). Paul shows that it was divine
patience that had permitted a temporary suspension of sin's
punishment prior to the Cross (Rom. 3:25). In the same way
both Old and New Testaments see God's wrath increasingly
focused on the final Day of the Lord (Zeph. 3:8, 1 Thess. 1:10).
It *is* being revealed now (Rom. 1:18), but not in full measure.
The function of the state is to execute God's wrath against all
wrong-doing (Rom. 13:4). While the State is to fulfil this task
impartially for the community, the individual Christian is to
shun taking revenge over personal grudges and animosities. God
is the ultimate judge; therefore 'leave it to the wrath of God'
(Rom. 12:19).

The life and teaching of Jesus are the best commentary on the
subject. Witness his combination of anger and grief at the hard-
ness of men's hearts (Mark 3:5). Consider the perfect control of
his wrath as he purged the Temple, that he had thought for the
protection of the doves from harm (John 2:15–16). Or contrast
the gracious invitation at the end of Matt. 11 with the woes upon
the cities just before it. No more solemn phrase does the Bible
contain than that of Rev. 6:16, 'The wrath of the Lamb'.